# WHO PRAYS for the PASTOR?

## Bro. Fredrick Ezeji-Okoye

Carpenter's Son Publishing

Who Prays for the Pastor?

Published by Carpenter's Son Publishing, Franklin, Tennessee

Published in association with Larry Carpenter of Christian Book Services, LLC
www.christianbookservices.com

Sites referred to within the text were retrieved prior to *Who Prays for the Pastor?* being printed. Author not responsible for sites no longer being available.

Cover and Interior Design by Adept Content Solutions

Printed in the United States of America

ISBN: 978-1-946889-48-5

# CONTENTS

# FOREWORD

*By Dr. Pastor Isaac Paintsil and Gregory Lanre Ijiwola, PhD*

## Dr. Pastor Isaac Paintsil

*Who Prays for the Pastor?* What a soul-searching question to
an ageless situation that many a church and a child of God
intentionally or unintentionally push to the outer recesses
of their minds in their life of faith! The work of the pastor,
which straddles the spiritual and earthly realms, serving
God according to His perfect will and translating that
service to human beings on the earth, is in my experience
and humble opinion, far more challenging than that of the
physician.

The work of the pastor is exceptionally complex but
unfathomably rewarding. To help you appreciate the intri-
cacy of the vocation, allow me to attempt a one-day snapshot
into the life of a pastor with an average-sized congregation.
A pastor prays for endless hours to be in a position to hear
the voice of God for His work and people distinctly. He
engages in endless study of and meditation on the dynamic
word of God, which gives a fresh revelation every time. He
indulges the complexity of juggling the limited time of each
day with a spouse, children, natural families, church families,
and the myriad functions of the work of ministry. Add to
this the endless hours officiating weddings, the dedication of

children, funerals, and other services; wearing multiple hats as manager, counselor, teacher, judge, and often janitor and babysitter; and much more that space would not permit me to enumerate.

In the pages of this insightful book, one of the finest servants of God that I have had the pleasure of knowing and working with, Brother Frederick Ezeji-Okoye, gives every child of God a peek into the rewarding but extremely challenging work of the pastors and ministers of God ordained as shepherds and bishops of the souls of countless children of God and churches all over the world.

In this age, when many men and women of God clamor for titles and degrees to bolster their legitimacy in ministry, Brother Fred, as he is affectionately called, has maintained strongly that he is not a pastor, apostle, teacher, or prophet; but called to serve pastors and those in the five-fold ministries. He is a rare gift of God in the Kingdom of God in our generation, with an unalloyed passion for the Lord Jesus Christ and serving the ministers of God.

Dr. Pastor Isaac Paintsil, MD, MPH, FACP, FHM, is the Senior Pastor of Christ's Oasis Ministries and Senior Attending Physician at John H. Stroger Jr. Hospital of Cook County, Chicago, Illinois.

★★★

## Gregory Lanre Ijiwola, PhD

Having pastored for about 27 years now, and also being a friend to many pastors around the world, I can fully identify with the subject of this book. As I read the manuscript, my mind raced back through certain moments in ministry when I felt that the last thing I wanted to do was continue. Those were moments of discouragement over testing events in ministry, times of internal agony over seemingly delayed visions and words from God, feeling crushed over financial needs of ministry, weariness over dealing with difficult individuals, juggling family and ministry priorities, temptations, feelings of self-doubt, conflicts, and so much more.

So how are pastors, who are supposed to be healers, be spiritually healthy enough, and effective in ministry, when they carry these burdens incessantly with no one to share them? Who are pastors to tell when they are struggling with their prayer lives or having continual conflicts with their spouses? Some pastors have tried confiding in congregation members and have lost their places or credibility. Some tried to pour out their burdens on their spouses and ended up overburdening their marriages to the detriment of their relationships with their spouses.

What does the pastor then do? Frederick, in this book, has done an amazing job in first bringing these issues to light in great details. I have known Fred for many years, and I have been a beneficiary of the heart God has given him to see to the health of pastors. He lives this passion every day, and many pastors can testify to how his ministry has been the final bulwark between them and giving up in ministry. Through the ministry of Men of Faith Network and other initiatives geared toward leaders, he is being used by God as a helper to me and many pastors in providing connections, encouragement, and support when it is available nowhere else. This compassionate heart he has is what bleeds through to you as you read *Who Prays for the Pastor?* It spoke deeply to my heart, and I believe it will speak to yours too.

I highly recommend this book for all pastors and those who would love to know how to help these heroes of the kingdom, who, though often misunderstood, misjudged, and criticized, sacrifice so much for the care of God's sheep and the advancement of God's kingdom on earth.

Gregory Lanre Ijiwola, PhD, is the Lead Pastor of The CityLight Church International, Chicago, Illinois

## What Pastors Are Saying

"I found myself crying uncontrollably and out loud!"

—Frederick K. Ezeji-Okoye

This statement was thought-provoking. I concluded that there are few things that best describe Hebrews 5:4 ("And no man taketh this honour unto himself, but he that is called of God, as was Aaron") than the burden God has given Evangelist Frederick K Ezeji-Okoye. A burden for the shepherds. *Who Prays for the Pastor?* is God-breathed as it addresses an infrequently discussed but important aspect of ministry life.

*Who Prays for the Pastor?* is a book that makes the non-ministers in our midst aware of the humanness of pastors. It also is a source of encouragement for the pastor to remain steadfast, the discouraged to keep on trying, and the fallen away to return.

By and large, the real-life testimonies of the author and others that he has shared make for encouraging reading. In doing so, Evangelist Fredrick displays the same vulnerability that he says is essential for the minister of the gospel.

I have personally taken the first step by reading this book twice over, and I have typed, framed, and hung the following from the book onto my office wall:

"Don't give up Pastor! Don't throw in the towel. There is renewed strength and vigor waiting for you in the presence of God. Your joy is filled, your peace is increased, your vision is clear."

—Frederick K Ezeji-Okoye

—Apostle JD Kosita-Madu

*Senior Pastor, Trinity Worship Centre (Beautiful Life Community)*
*Rector, Sterling Faith School Of Ministry and Christian Leadership*

★★★

*Who Prays for the Pastor?* by Fredrick Ezeji-Okoye encourages prayer, understanding, and support for ministers. It discusses many of the needs pastors and ministers may have, as well as some pitfalls and dangers to avoid. I especially enjoyed the section on forgiveness.

—Dr. Tony McCanless

★★★

*Who Prays for the Pastor?* is an eye-opener, a must-read by all members of every Living Church. Pastors keep giving until sometimes they have nothing left to give. I challenge both ministers and congregants to read this revolutionary book to enable our churches to be strengthened again through intercession for their pastors. *Who Prays for the Pastor?* is essential for discovering the blessing we receive by praying for pastors and the damage we cause by not praying for them.

—Pastor Foster Tsagil

★★★

Driven by his compassion for pastors, Fred has revealed uniquely the causes of frustrations among pastors, and practical ways of avoiding such pitfalls. The work is very mandatory to every servant of God.

—Pastor Alex Emmanuel

★★★

Evangelist Fred presents a summarized peek at God's chosen ones. There's an alignment between this work and similar challenging encounters of Prophet Elijah (1 Kings 19:3). And yet, *Who Prays for the Pastor?* posits practical steps for a victorious lifestyle for God's chosen ones, especially examples of daily living and guiding principles. This book is chronicled in revelation—therefore—a must-read!

—Dr. Godfrey Ekhomu, CPA

★★★

This great book is irresistible! The brilliance and the author's choice of materials will aid everyone to rightly petition God for their leaders and those whom they love. Highly recommended!

—Pastor Vincent Ehigie

***

*Who Prays for the Pastor?* We have in our hands an excellent tool for the ministry, not just for pastors but for all believers in Christ—for we are all called to serve. It is a book inspired from above, backed with the practical and personal experience of our brother. It blessed my soul and will bless yours too. I pray that God will use it to raise people of faith who will pray for pastors.

—Ven. Dr. Paul Enwonwu

***

When God calls, He equips, enables, provides, and qualifies such that the person called can fight a good fight, finish the race, and keep the faith. Unfortunately many pastors today are experiencing spiritual burnout and other experiences such as criticism, betrayal, divorce and broken homes, unruly children, rejection, unfruitfulness, and loneliness. *Who Prays for the Pastor?* expounds on a number of secret pains that pastors go through on their journey to answering the call of God to pastor His people. It also brings to light the fact that pastors are not on this journey alone and need not die quietly in their pains. When you read this book, as a pastor, you will be encouraged that the One who called you into ministry will surely see you to the end, if you abide in Him. *Who Prays for the Pastor?* is a question that should not be shrugged off. As a congregation, you will be encouraged by this book always to find time to pray for your pastors, protect your pastors, encourage your pastors, and support their work.

I hereby recommend this book to both pastors and church members.

—Pastor Ben Nnebechukwu, Uganda

★★★

*Who Prays for the Pastor?* is a book that not only breaks the myth about the superhuman abilities of pastors but exposes their human frailties. They fall sick as we do; they commit sin, suffer emotional breakdown, and, above all, are the chief targets of constant satanic attacks to derail their ministries. This book was written to encourage and motivate congregants to pray for their pastors and for pastors to get help by associating with fellow pastors in a forum where they can be encouraged, mentored, and supported to fulfill their assignments.

—Rev. Chuma Okorafor

★★★

*Who Prays for the Pastor?* delivers powerful testimony coinciding a message the entire body of Christ needs to hear. The importance of prayer for pastors is vital if we want a successful congregation that responds in unison with the Spirit of God. Frederick touches on meaningful subjects, and I found myself writing down quotes to utilize in my everyday walk with God. Excellent work!

—Tiffanie Chappell

★★★

I truly believe this book, *Who Prays for the Pastor?*, will help leaders and pastors in active ministry and other professions. The title and contents are challenging to realities of many of today's leaders, including myself. I trust that those who will read and use the principles contained in this book will experience an uncommon turnaround in ministry and life.

—Pastor John Eshiba

★★★

The Man of God Fredrick K. Ezeji-Okoye has thoroughly hit the nail on the head with his thought-provoking insights and Holy Spirit–inspired discernment on so many levels concerning the pastorate. If ever we pastors needed prayer before, we earthen vessels sure do need it now. His no-nonsense, down-to-business approach is tempered with grace, compassion, and wisdom, and is forged in experience! The book will prove to be a refreshing, cold drink to every thirsty pastor—and if you are not thirsty yet, keep on pastoring!

—Pastor Mel Keyes

\*\*\*

The church is engulfed in warfare, and ministers of the Gospel are leading the charge. Not even the best minister will be left standing if he does not receive the covering fire which is the prayer of the saints. The cry and plea of Apostle Paul in Ephesians 6:19, "Pray for me …," is the cry of every minister. The author has passionately reviewed areas of struggle for ministers. Become acquainted with the issues of your minister so that you can be his Aaron or Hur. Your minister will be what you make him, through your prayer for him—or lack of it.

—Rev. Sunday Bwanhot, Missionary/Pastor, Chicago

\*\*\*

I greatly enjoyed reading the insightful and practical truths from a man who understands the call, the function, and the burden of pastors. Evangelist Fredrick K. Ezeji-Okoye has faithfully served pastors for many years in the areas of intercession, exhortation, and encouragement, and provides a monthly platform of accountability and fellowship for pastors through the Men of Faith Network, where he serves as President. Evangelist Ezeji-Okoye transparently addresses critical issues dear to the hearts of pastors, with clarity, accuracy, and balance. This book will certainly bless both laity and clergy, and assist you in understanding not only "Who" but "How to" pray for the pastor.

—Dr. Ray Allen Berryhill, Chicago

★★★

Bro. Fredrick Ezeji-Okoye has written an amazing book for every pastor to add to their library! As a pastor, I felt strengthened, encouraged, corrected, and renewed while reading this manuscript. The wisdom and compassion of God exude through every chapter. Absolutely a must-read for every new pastor and for any pastor dealing with discouragement or entering into a new season of ministry. You will walk away with practical wisdom and tools to apply to your everyday life. *Who Prays for the Pastor?* will change how you lead and how you serve.

—Pastor Shonda V. Burns, Chicago

★★★

Transparency and authenticity are two qualities of the Kingdom that are incredibly important and often lacking. In the book *Who Prays for the Pastor?* Evangelist Fred does not beat around the bush; he is straightforward, and with precept and example, with humility and transparency, he addresses major areas of concern with us pastors. The trait I like most is Fred's transparency and examples of personal repentance. The personal stories add impact and relevance and will encourage self-examination in the heart of any conscious leader.

—Pastor Kelvin Easter

★★★

I am very grateful to the Lord God Most High for this book, *Who Prays for the Pastor?* I cannot agree more because this came to Brother Fredrick Ezeji-Okoye by revelation from God, and he has written from his personal experience as a minister of the Gospel. The content is masterfully written for the servant of God to find help when it is needed the most. The book opened my eyes to the truth of the Word of God to live faithfully before God and man. Parishioners too will find delight in earnestly praying for their pastor, rather than fault-finding and ungodly accusations. To God alone be all the glory.

—Pastor Michael C. Mordi, Minnesota

★★★

Authentic, real, raw, deep, and filled with a compassionate point of view, *Who Prays for the Pastor?* is a unique inside view from a pastor's heart. It's a compelling read for parishioners and pastors, both of whom will benefit from this spirit-filled book.

—Terri Bradley

★★★

*Who Prays for the Pastor?* is born out of years of agonizing over the plight of God's ministers. This work details the unfortunate and unenviable circumstances of men of God who spend their entire lives pouring out their all for their congregations: praying, counseling, serving, ministering—while virtually being left at the mercy of wolves because no one bothers to intercede for them.

The author suggests and affirms strongly that men of God equally deserve to be prayed for and also ministered to on a regular basis, and therefore advocates that congregation members make a conscious and determined effort to make intercession for these servants of God.

Well thought-out, well written, and amply illustrated, *Who Prays for the Pastor?* is a timely work, particularly in this season when true ministers of God are under so much pressure to deliver. This book will bring great encouragement and hope to all who have been called of God to serve in any capacity in these last days. This is a must-read for every minister.

—Pastor Conrad Oseibonsu

★★★

*Who Prays for the Pastor?* is an excellent read for everyone who considers pursuing or continuing their call to the pastorate. In this text, Brother Frederick Ezeji-Okoye uses personal experience coupled with the scriptures in a compelling way that provides healing for those who have been wounded while contending for the souls of men, or as a warning of how to avoid the entrapments that have befallen many pastors. Brother Frederick begins this journey by providing us with an essential component for successful ministry: developing and maintaining continuous, unbroken fellowship with the Lord, the authentic Vine. I am reminded of Mark 3:14: "And he appointed twelve (whom he also named apostles) so that they might be with him and he might send them out to preach." Being with Him should always precede any attempt of ministry. Thank you, Brother Frederick, for such an insightful work!

—Bishop Arthur Guice, Senior Pastor

★★★

Being human is vulnerability at its best! Being a pastor is a calling to live out vulnerability and not fail. This book reveals the truth of the calling of a pastor and how to succeed beyond vulnerability in the power of Christ's love.

—Dr. Joseph Rhoiney, Ministry ONE

★★★

Evangelist Fred has absolutely delivered a sober and timeless gift of wisdom to the body of Christ. If your assignment is that of shepherding a local assembly, then this book has been written just for you. Your relationship with God and that of your spouse, your family, your church family, as well as the destiny of your ministry, will never be the same.

—Pastor Greg Morris

★★★

Pastors have challenges and struggles just like every other human being. But often they don't have anyone interceding for them as they do for their congregants, family, and friends. This book, *Who Prays for the Pastor?*, highlights the numerous struggles and challenges that most pastors go through, enlightens readers on the importance of praying for their pastors, and more importantly, empowers the pastor on how to stay strong and win at any of life's challenges, including discouragement and being overwhelmed in ministry.

—Rev. Nonnie Roberson

# INTRODUCTION

One Sunday morning in the winter of 2009 my pastor, at the time, was praying. He prayed passionately for the sick and declared blessings over the congregation. Standing right beside him as he prayed, I suddenly heard a still small voice asking me, *Who prays for the pastor?* As an ordained evangelist working directly with the pastor, I knew of his challenges, but I didn't know exactly why God asked, *Who prays for the pastor?* I felt so heavy at that moment. Despite my pastor's various issues (ongoing and unresolved), he was present Sunday after Sunday, service after service, praying his heart out and asking God's blessings upon the congregation.

On the ride home that Sunday afternoon with my family, I found myself crying uncontrollably and out loud, like a baby. My wife became worried and asked me what the problem was. I had no choice but to share with her the sudden burden that came upon me as I heard God ask me, *Who prays for the pastor?* She encouraged me, as any good wife should. However, I still could not answer God's question. Over time, I pondered the question more and more, praying diligently for clarity. After about six months, God put the long-awaited clarity in my heart. He was looking for more than just one person (me) praying for my pastor. It was something larger than my local

pastor, something greater than me. God was calling for ministry to pastors on a larger scale.

There is a part of pastors that few take time to consider.
No matter how humble the pastor, he will not be able to fully
present himself to the congregation for prayer, disclosing his
most trying experiences. Even if he gathered the courage to
divulge personal challenges and ask the congregation to pray,
he risks losing the confidence of the people he is leading.
Many pastors keep things private (one reason they can become
isolated) for fear of their followers seeing them sweat, or
witnessing them in their weakest moments. Might such vulnerability result in church members doubting the faith their
pastor so fervently teaches? Could this level of exposure cause
them to lose hope? Can the pastor's authenticity provoke fear
in the people, and eventually cause them to scatter? Might it
be possible, in a pastor's mind, that such vulnerability, exposure, and authenticity is a type of "striking the pastor, causing
the sheep to scatter?" What pastor, in his right mind, would
do such a thing?

# MEN OF FAITH NETWORK

Thank God for the grace to hear Him speak and the grace to understand what He is saying. I listened to the Lord as He was talking to my heart: "Gather pastors. Create a platform for them to come together in one accord to worship, pray, hear words of exhortation, and encourage one another." As I received His words, I felt peace, a confirming peace that God had spoken to me. Only now, how would I commence this task for God?

Finally, by His grace, I gathered the courage in September 2009 to invite six pastors and leaders to hear my assignment. Five honored the invitation, and I had an acknowledgment of support from the sixth. I shared the vision and the importance of creating a platform where pastors would assemble monthly, in one accord, to worship God in spirit and truth. By the grace of God, the birth of that vision is known today as the Men of Faith Network. To date, this network has been, and still is, a life-changing experience for pastors and leaders.

Pastors benefit from connecting with other pastors and leaders, experiencing authentic fellowship, and divesting themselves of titles and pomp. Leaders who attend experience this during the Men of Faith Network gatherings. Pastors come in without wearing their titles and are free to express themselves to God in worship, hear the word of truth, and pray for one another.

Parishioners should share the burden of praying for our pastors. Week after week, we come to receive that which God has poured into them. We have many expectations of them, expressed and unexpressed. We even place demands on our pastors, such as requests to pray for us, to officiate family weddings, to eulogize our loved ones... The list goes on. How often does the average congregant stop to consider the pastor's needs? If the pastor is doing all the pouring, how is he being replenished? Do we play a role in the advancement and the decline of our local pastors? It is time to become the ones who pray for our pastors.

We often hear stories of fallen pastors, whether in cases of fraudulence, adultery, fornication, child abuse, or divorce. Suicide also seems to be prevalent among pastors. Isolation, division, sickness, inability to provide for their families, unfruitful ministry, lack of souls won to the cross, and lack of spiritual fathering and mentoring can eventually lead to pastors walking away from their pulpits, perhaps walking away defeated. Where will they go? What will they do? Will they recover? Will congregants care? *Who prays for the pastor?*

The purpose of this book is to bring awareness to many things pastors experience on their journeys to answering the call of God to shepherd His people, to encourage pastors to connect with like-minded leaders for fellowship, accountability, and spiritual development. I hope that pastors will read the final words of this book and feel refreshed in knowing that God is the God of mercy and grace. King David penned it well: "Even though I walk through the valley of the shadow of death, I will fear no evil, for you are with me; your rod and your staff, they comfort me" (Psalm 23:4). I pray that this book will encourage you to remain holy in the course of your assignment, fully understanding that God who gives vision also makes the provision. God told Habakkuk plainly, "Though the vision tarries, it will surely come to pass" (Habakkuk 2:3).

For the pastors who have fallen or walked away from your assignments, be strong and courageous. Repent from your heart, reconnect to the Father of grace, mercy, and unconditional love, knowing that God accepts you as His beloved. Consider Peter and Judas. Both disciples committed the same sin, betraying Jesus. However, Peter repented and went on to become the leading apostle of the New Testament Church. Judas, on the other hand, could not live with his sin, choosing suicide in place of grace.

For congregants and those who support pastors, *Who Prays for the Pastor?* will open your eyes and, by the grace of God, you will experience a revelation of the importance of interceding for the pastors connected to you. Understanding what pastors, including yours, experience (or can experience) should provoke more passion to interact with them as humans and not angels or mini-gods. This book will also stir your spirit to extend grace for pastors who have erred or sinned along the way—not to kill them with your words, but to restore them with your prayers and intercession. Imagine those who knew of David's sin—and never gave him space for God's grace. He repented and was reconciled to God after adultery with Bathsheba and the murder scandal of Uriah. We often see people fall but rarely recognize their reconciliation. Psalm 51 shows David's true repentance from his heart. No wonder God referred to him as a man after His own heart. What is in your heart for your pastor?

## Chapter 1
# FINDING BALANCE

*"I am the vine; you are the branches. Whoever abides in me and I in him, he it is that bears much fruit, for apart from me you can do nothing. If anyone does not abide in me he is thrown away like a branch and withers; and the branches are gathered, thrown into the fire, and burned." (John 15: 5–6)*

Stress is common among pastors as they carry out their various assignments. In many instances, members of their congregations are unaware of the stress and have no idea of its impact on them. Unfortunately, misguided beliefs exist on both sides. Congregants tend to feel that their pastor should be available to them whenever needed. Likewise, pastors seem to believe they have to be available for church members as needed. These beliefs and subsequent behaviors tend to add to the pastor's stress load. Pastors deserve time away from their local churches to be themselves without feeling overwhelmed by the demands of the church and its members. Quality time with the Lord is necessary for pastors as they recover during the week between scheduled services and other pastoral obligations.

In John 15:5, Jesus presents a simple truth: "I am the vine; you are the branches. Whoever abides in me and I in him, he it is that bears much fruit, for apart from me you can do nothing." Jesus emphasizes connectedness between Himself and His followers. This connection has no different meaning for pastors, who too are followers of Christ. Pastors must remain connected to the Vine to receive from God as it provides strength, nourishment, and revelation to carry out this particular assignment.

Coupled with the many methods and resources available for a pastor, he has to have the revelation of what God has called him to. Church planting and leadership strategies are important for pastors and church leaders, but a full understanding of, and total surrender to, the call is necessary for the pastor to thrive. Structure and strategy are required, but God, I believe, gives each pastor and local congregation their uniqueness. Having a particular anointing upon a church is a great reason for pastors to connect directly to the Vine.

Years ago, while serving a local church as an ordained evangelist, I wore many hats. I was in charge of the intercessory prayer line as well as conducting Wednesday night services and Friday vigils. I went from one Saturday program to another, from one Sunday service to another, and from meeting to meeting. Oh, I also worked a full-time job, outside of the church, to provide for my wife and children.

I recall coming home from work, looking forward to the intercessory prayer line that usually lasted an hour, most times longer. Afterward, I often found myself exhausted and ready for bed, having spent no time with my wife and children! My priorities were misplaced, and I was losing those most important to me. God expects ministry to take place at home first!

In the midst of working the ministry, I found that I had become bitter and angry, lacking peace and joy. I struggled with health issues, and I was always stressed out. It also affected my marriage, which I will share fully in the next chapter. I could not understand why things were going wrong all around my family and me, while those I prayed for were continually giving testimonies of answered prayers.

The more I ran around doing the work of the church, the more stressed I became. The workload at the church continued to increase. Not long after, there was division among the leadership. God is not an author of confusion. How can we work so hard in the ministry, yet we have no peace? I am reminded of Mary and Martha when Jesus visited their home. Martha focused on the business of the home, while Mary focused her attention on Jesus. Both matters were important. However, Jesus pointed out the one thing they needed most: to receive from Him. I had the mindset of Martha, focusing on "church work" when I should have been focusing on connecting to the Vine first, allowing Jesus to guide my next steps.

## The Importance of Quality Time

During a Men of Faith Network monthly gathering, one of the speakers addressed the importance of ministers' prayer lives. He talked about how some ministers keep busy ministry calendars but lack personal prayer lives and relationships with God. It was as if the man of God knew my schedule and was speaking directly to me. By that point, I felt like Prophet Isaiah felt when he said, "I am a man of unclean lips." I was free at that moment! I returned home and instantly adjusted my schedule. I recognized the importance of keeping the fire of my altar burning. Spending personal time with God helped me put things in perspective and gain clarity of God's will for my life. The more time I spend with God, the more balanced I am, and the more strength I have.

Spending time with God is a time of fellowship, time to worship Him for who He is. It is a time for me to honor and praise Him. It's a time to read for spiritual growth and be silent before Him to hear a word that will make a difference. I have come to realize that I achieve much during quality time with the Lord.

Quality time is the foundation that will determine the height of one's ministry. The foundation of a building is key to the strength of the structure built upon it. The deeper the foundation, the higher and stronger the building will be. The same applies to our relationships with God. Jesus is our best role model. He understood and incorporated the wisdom of personal quality time with the Father in His days on earth. Although He spent much time with the disciples and multitudes, Jesus consistently separated himself to pray alone in the mountains. This time alone was Jesus' way of maintaining His relationship with His foundation, God. Mark gives an example of this in Mark 6:46: "And after he had taken leave of them, he went up on the mountain to pray." Luke records another time in Luke 6:12-13, "In these days he went out to the mountain to pray, and all night he continued in prayer to God. And when day came, he called his disciples and chose from them twelve, whom he named apostles." If Jesus applied this principle, it is essential that we do the same.

## Effective Leaders

When a pastor carries out his assignment with ineffective leaders, he becomes overwhelmed! Choosing leaders can be challenging. Weak leaders have done more harm than good for the pastor. Arguments, misunderstandings, and delegated, unaccomplished assignments become the order of the day. A pastor is supposed to assign tasks and consider them done, not finding himself doing the work. To avoid such, it is important for pastors to prayerfully choose effective leaders who will help them carry out God's work.

Pastors are responsible for building leaders just as Jesus built His disciples. It is important for pastors to connect with their leaders, as this connection becomes the vein for training those who lead and strengthening their potential. However, if the runners (leaders) refuse to run with the vision, they create an imbalance in the local church. This lack of balance creates problems and hinders the advancement of the assignment.

Pastors benefit from a well-organized, structured local church. Choosing leaders is paramount to moving the vision of the church forward. Much like Jesus, pastors have to choose those whom they can trust with the vision, as well as the responsibility to make it happen. Pastors should receive vision from God while in His presence. It is God's responsibility to give the vision. Your responsibility, pastor, is to publish it for the runners, who will carry the vision to the masses.

To conclude, be reminded that without God, we can do nothing. Our connection to the Father has to remain tight. The only way is to stay connected to Christ. Let John 15:5–6 become key verses in the back of our minds regardless of calling: we are branches, and Jesus is the Vine. The more of Jesus in us, the more strength, wisdom, knowledge, understanding, love, power, joy, peace, and more! Even amidst stressful lives, there is a balance God will allow us to achieve, especially when we stay connected.

## Chapter 2

# ORDER OF FAMILY

*"Whoever troubles his own household will inherit the wind, and the fool will be servant to the wise of heart." (Proverbs 11:29)*

### The Marriage

I love the testimony of one of God's generals whose wife had a problem with him, which led to her requesting a divorce. Their story shocked the Christian community, and it affected his personal ministry. Thank God, by His grace they reunited.

This man never believed his wife would go to that extent until it happened. He confessed that he felt ministry should be the priority before family, which is what he taught others. He had a "God-first" ministry. This pastor conducted crusade after crusade. The testimonies of miracles were numerous. Seeing God work through him on this level, he did not stop to consider the fact that his family was falling apart. The expectation was for them to follow him and continue to witness God's hand through ministry. Unfortunately, his wife became overwhelmed and could no longer endure the pressure of his lack of commitment to her and their children. What got this pastor's attention? Reading the divorce papers his wife filed. In his mind, he was doing everything right. After all, God was working through him! By God's grace, this pastor internalized the divorced request and reconciled with his wife and family. He currently has a more impactful ministry, only now with proper focus and structure. Many pastors in divorce situations experience great emotional difficulty. However, pastors have to do whatever it takes to maintain balance and peace within the home and family structure.

Hearing the testimony of this pastor forced me to reconsider my own relationships with my wife, children, and ministry. My spirit became stirred, and my eyes became wide open. As I mentioned in chapter one, I had become so consumed with ministry work that I could not see how I was neglecting my family. I did not see anything wrong; after all, I considered the work of God first. This faulty thinking caused a lot of unrest in my home.

My wife and I had many disagreements, due primarily to my lack of commitment. I remember coming home one day, seeing the house in disarray, and yelling at the top of my voice. I went upstairs to use the restroom. Washing my hands, I saw my reflection in the mirror staring back at me. I looked horrible. The Holy Spirit convicted me on how I lived a double life. Outside of my home, I was known as a gentle and soft-spoken evangelist! But in my house, I had a different reputation.

I reflected and realized that if I did not readjust, I too might receive a life-altering divorce letter. Thank God for the grace of obedience.

Prioritizing my family before ministry restored peace in my home. Spending time with my wife and children, practicing what I preach at home and having everyone live in one accord made a huge difference. Two cannot walk together except they agree. Pastors have to agree with their spouses to bring rest at home so that their ministry will reflect the glory of God. No matter how gifted you are, without family tranquility, the beauty of God is not revealed through your ministry. We ought to encourage one another and ourselves by acknowledging the truth that God honors marriage and family.

A peaceful marriage and home limits stress for pastors because it provides a place for solace and support. It is important for pastors to fully understand God's original order for family and Kingdom ministry. God is not the author of confusion; His plans always include clarity, direction, and balance. Paul teaches this very plainly in Ephesians 5 when he writes concerning God's order for ministry.

## The Children

Pastors need quality time with their families. There are far too many adults raised in church who have since left and are no longer following Christ. More often than not, it has been due to poor examples of "pastor-parents" and feeling the need to compete with the church for their parents' attention.

Pastors' children are often under pressure. All eyes are on them, watching to see how or where they will fail as a pastor's kid. Pastors sometimes neglect the care and nurture of their children because of the ministry workload. Many times pastors expect their children to attend all church programs. The average pastor wants his family to be involved in the local church. As a result, the children are expected to attend weekly Bible study, be in the choir, learn musical instruments, and complete other tasks no one else has committed to perform. Do pastors set the bar too high for their families? Are they sometimes inconsiderate of their family's time, talents, and commitments?

Unfortunately, many of these pastors' children grow up without personal relationships with God because all their days have been under pressure to work in the church. The moment they reach adolescence, they rebel and often become the opposite of who their parents are, or who their parents expected them to become. This change causes much unrest in the family and negatively impacts the calling of the pastor's family!

Nothing hurts a pastor more than seeing his children become worthless in the Kingdom. How ironic it is for a pastor to see his spiritual children doing well in the Kingdom while his natural children, in some cases, flourish in the world's kingdom.

Pastors should to do their best and allow the Holy Spirit help them raise their families. Children learn from what they see. They follow by influence and not by force. If we preach about loving one another and avoiding malice, but at home the pastor demonstrates the opposite, the children are indeed receiving a different message. If there is a place to live our Christian life, it should be at home. Setting our priorities right and doing what we teach at home should be the way of life we model. By God's grace, our children will grow up and do the same.

However, things don't just happen. Pastors will benefit from devoting more time to bringing and maintaining order and spiritual development in their homes. Consider the power of individual and family prayer. Of course, children should see their "pastor-parents" praying in the home and spending quality time with the Lord. This sets a great example before them. Also, pastors should spend time teaching their children the meaning and importance of prayer, while praying along with them regularly. Prayer prepares the heart to know God, and it should be the desire of all pastors that their children know God.

## The Ministry

Let's conclude this chapter by emphasizing the negligence that pastors demonstrate toward ministry due to family priorities. Most often, leaders are faced with challenges carrying out God's assignment committed in their hands. God wants us to lead our families diligently and likewise the ministry. Struggling with knowing when to work or take a vacation, when to pay a compassionate visit to a church member or stay home with family, when to delegate taking ad-hoc phone calls from church members should not happen.

God is not the author of confusion. He orders the steps of the righteous. As long as we abide in Him, as mentioned in chapter one, finding balance and maintaining the integrity of our hearts in serving God faithfully, He will always preserve us from the mistakes experienced through negligence. He will give us wisdom to properly set our priorities and redeem the timing correctly. Knowing what to say and saying it at the right time, or knowing what to do and doing it at the right time, should be the grace pastors need to avoid negligence in their ministry. Jesus knew exactly what to say and do when He was faced with family conflict and the ministry. He understood God's timing, and that helped Him avoid the offer to turn from ministry toward His family (Luke 2:42–51). Jesus respected both family and ministry. However, He knew the art of balance and the value of prioritizing. We, too, can achieve both.

## Chapter 3
# DISCOURAGEMENT

*"And David was greatly distressed; for the people spake of stoning him, because the soul of all the people was grieved, every man for his sons and for his daughters: but David encouraged himself in the Lord his God." (1 Samuel 30:6)*

I stood in front of the congregation and testified that my wife had conceived and was pregnant with a baby! Praise and worship filled the sanctuary, because we were overdue to have a second child, and many were expecting such news. We celebrated the goodness of our Lord Jesus, and I encouraged those believing God for babies to hold on to their faith. In fact, I prayed from my heart, with confidence and boldness, for those who were anticipating fruit of the womb. So many were blessed and went home encouraged.

A few days later, I received an emergency call at work, requesting me to come immediately to Northwestern's Women's Hospital. There, I found my wife rolling on the floor and weeping uncontrollably. I could not understand what was going on, until the nurse walked up, pulled me to the side, and told me of their intention to abort the baby in the womb and the reasons behind the decision. My task was to convince my wife to agree to this ruling against her wish.

Here I was, a minister of faith, torn between standing by my wife and standing with the report of the medical team.

Finally, I had a word from the Lord and said it out loud for my wife to hear: "Let go! The future is greater." That was the word she needed to hear, and indeed, she let go. They took her into the operating room to terminate the pregnancy. Driving home later that evening was miserable and depressing. We felt so discouraged, disappointed, and ashamed. On the way, I kept asking God, "How do I explain to the church what happened?" I could not comprehend it.

For days, it was a great struggle for us. Our home was not peaceful. As for me, I did not feel like attending service the next Sunday. Not because I had lost hope in God, but because I did not know how to face the congregation. As for my wife, she could not understand why this would be God's will for us. This is a woman who had suffered the loss of her mother and a brother within two years. Now, just about five years later, she experienced the loss of our unborn child. Understand, we had tried for several years to have a second child. She felt empty and disgusted. During that time her countenance changed. My wife felt that I was responsible for her losing the baby. She argued that I had shared our testimony openly to the church, exposing her and the baby to the enemy. There was nothing I could say. No explanation I could offer would make sense to her. I felt isolated from my wife, alone and discouraged.

During the same week, I received telephone calls from congregants who needed prayer. One call was to come to the hospital and pray for someone who had just been admitted. As physically and spiritually depleted as I was, I went to the hospital. When I returned home, I felt strength from nowhere, a supernatural replenishing. Though the peace between my wife and me had not been restored, I drew from the Word, "But David encouraged himself in the Lord his God" (1 Samuel 30:6).

There will be times when pastors will face challenges that their family members will not understand. At such a time there seems to be no one to encourage them. Pastors, too, have to encourage themselves. I had no option but to encourage myself by remembering the goodness of God in my life, how God had brought me so far—and I declared that my Lord is great. I laid aside every weight, looking unto Jesus, the author and finisher of my faith.

My moving forward with patience, hope, and faith reconnected my wife and me. Before we knew it, our next baby had arrived! We named her Nkiruka ("the future is greater"). Another baby, Chinenye ("God gives"), arrived unexpectedly within the space of two years, and we found ourselves going for family planning.

Pastors, regardless of what you experience, you must remind yourself that God has the final say! Encourage yourself when nobody seems to understand what you are going through. It is a myth that pastors are never discouraged. Job had to encourage himself when even his wife could not figure out why he kept his integrity. We need to confess the Word that will stir our spirit, hear the words that will maintain a burning fire, and always inquire of the Lord. After David encouraged himself, he gained momentum to ask the Lord for guidance. The Lord responded to David in 1 Samuel 30:8: "Pursue: for thou shalt surely overtake them, and without fail recover all." Having God on our side will always help us to get back everything that was taken.

## Sources of Discouragement

Most of the things that happen to pastors happen for a purpose. Understanding the test of faith is crucial. James said to count it all joy when we pass through trials and tribulation. It does not make sense, yet it is true. Our ways and God's ways are not the same; His thoughts and ours are not the same. Pastors get discouraged seeing the opposite of what they preach happen to them. It is challenging, for instance, to see how a preacher with so much anointing to heal others gets sick and is admitted to the hospital.

The Bible never made clear the meaning of the thorn in Paul's flesh. Paul said he prayed three good times that the Lord might remove the thorn, but God did not. All he got was the sufficient grace to ride on. There are many things we may not understand, but we need this same grace. The Bible recorded that even before Jesus started his ministry, he was led by the Spirit to be tempted by the devil. Jesus passed the test, and the devil left for a season. We must continually depend on the grace of God to pass each test.

*Rejection* is a familiar source of discouragement for pastors. I have learned that some pastors attempt to avoid rejection within their local churches by hand-selecting their "amen corner" and "yes people." Many have selected board members who will agree with whatever they propose. Some consider the potential of rejection when preparing sermons, and err on the side of what they feel the people want to hear, while rejecting that which God intends to speak through them. Pastor, not everyone will receive what God gives you, in vision or sermon. Luke 6:26 says, "Woe unto you, when all men shall speak well of you! For so did their father to the false prophets."

Pastors need to be led by the Holy Spirit, in word, in vision, and in action. Not everyone will agree with what God has given the pastor. Sometimes congregants will not see what he sees. Trying to pull everyone along with him can become discouraging. A strong pastor is one who has learned not to be passive in his approach to leadership. Confidence is a sure weapon against rejection. In chapter six, "Rejection," I discuss the topic in more detail, with ways to help pastors in this area.

Another source of discouragement is what some consider **unanswered prayers**. Unanswered prayers can be very disappointing and heartbreaking. Many of us do not seem to understand why God does not answer prayers the way we want Him to. One thing is certain: God answers all prayers! At times we can be selfish and self-centered in our requests to

God. Upon asking Him, many times we have already fixed our minds on the answer we want, obviously in what we believe to be our best interest. However, it is entirely unfair to God for us not to consider His willful, very purposeful response to such requests. This self-inflicted disappointment brings discouragement to many pastors.

God will not honor prayers according to our will, but God will honor prayers according to His will. Once we pray His will, we see the manifestation. I was invited to pray for a brother in the hospital. I stepped in with faith and prayed faith prayers with the young man's family. Guess what? The next day, the person who had invited me for that prayer called. Deep inside my heart, when I saw his call, I thought he was calling to give me the testimony of answered prayers, knowing fully well how God moved on the day I prayed for his younger family member. However, he called to let me know that the young man had passed that night. This scenario was not the first time I had received news opposite of what I prayed, and honestly, each time it happened, I became discouraged. Psalm 42:11 records, "Why art thou cast down, O my soul? And why art thou disquieted within me? Hope thou in God: for I shall yet praise him, who is the health of my countenance, and my God."

Speak positive words to encourage your soul when it is cast down. Whenever I find myself in such situations, instead of feeling discouraged, I have learned to confess positive scriptures and recall the many prayers God had already answered. Discouragement is not God's will for pastors or anyone else. I am learning more and more to be like Jesus. My confession to God is, "Father, let your will be done, not my will." For as many times as God's answers were contrary to my desires, there are more experiences where He answered exactly the way I wanted Him to. Either way, we serve a faithful, reliable, and dependable God.

*Comparison* is another trap that leads to discouragement. Most often, pastors fall into it unknowingly. Many pastors share experiences among one another, especially things that are working well in their churches. Pastor, please be fully aware of what God has called you to do! Take Pastor Mike and Pastor Lumbar (fictitious names), for example. The two met at a leadership conference. After exchanging their business cards, Pastor Lumbar decided to give Pastor Mike a call. During their conversation, he learned that Pastor Mike has 1,000 members in his church, while Pastor Lumbar has 200. Lumbar became increasingly interested in learning how to grow his church.

Pastor Lumbar arranged to meet Pastor Mike at his church. He learned so much from Pastor Mike. The two talked at length, sharing visions and experiences. One of Pastor Mike's suggestions was to beautify the temple as a method to increase membership. Pastor Lumbar left excited and ran with the idea. He secured a loan, using tips from Pastor Mike, spent it on refurbishing their church, then bought a new car as Pastor Mike advised. A few months later, rather than the church membership increasing, it was decreasing. Church members were no longer being fed spiritually, and many began facing financial pressure from the pastor and felt the only option was to leave.

Pastor Lumbar became discouraged because he detoured from God's path for him. Comparing himself to Pastor Mike led him right into the arms of discouragement. Anytime we leave our primary assignment to chase what has worked for others, we acquaint ourselves with discouragement: "For we dare not make ourselves of the number, or compare ourselves with some that commend themselves: but they measuring themselves by themselves, and comparing themselves among themselves, are not wise. But we will not boast of things without our measure, but according to the measure of the rule which God hath distributed to us, a measure to reach even unto you" (2 Corinthians 10:12–13).

*Unfruitfulness* has a way of causing many pastors to feel downcast. As much as we might profess not being interested in numbers, do not be deceived: increasing membership numbers are encouraging. Every pastor would like to experience growth in the ministry, as much as congregants would like to experience spiritual growth and physical blessings. The greatest joy of a pastor is seeing members blessed beyond measure! When this is not the case, discouragement yet again creeps in. We have to do what is necessary to take care of and nurture our congregations, but we must commit all into the hands of God.

Every pastor expects fruitfulness, and rightfully so. Pastors sow a tremendous amount of time into individuals and the working of the ministry. It is only human to expect fruit from their labors. After all, scripture does teach us to anticipate a harvest when we plant. The Lord stated that when we abide in Him, we shall become fruitful. He was with the disciples working with them, and many signs followed the disciples. It is natural for us to expect results. When we do not see them, we are more likely to become cast down.

We have to be very cautious of impatience. Sometimes it's not a matter of fruitfulness but rather a question of impatience. Many things planted, whether fruits, vegetables, or flowers, have an anticipated time of harvest. The harvest depends on what has been planted. Sometimes the harvest may come later than expected, but that does not mean the harvest is not coming. It is important for pastors to discern when more patience is needed. We have to move away from the "microwave" approach to ministry—we want something done, and we want it now! Daniel 10:1 tells us, "In the third year of Cyrus king of Persia a thing was revealed unto Daniel, whose name was called Belteshazzar; and the thing was true, but the time appointed was long: and he understood the thing, and had understanding of the vision." Daniel understood the timing.

For us, moments of discouragement come not because the vision is not true but because we missed the timing.

Pastors, remember one thing for sure: God will always make a way of escape in times of discouragement. He comforts you when you are cast down, allowing you to comfort others. Jesus told Peter that the devil was out to crush him but that He (Jesus) had prayed for Peter so he could go ahead and pray for others. So whenever discouragement manifests, remember that God is training you at that moment to enable you to pass the test, learn from it, and teach others. Any test of faith passed is always crowned with an unusual anointing.

## Chapter 4
# FORGIVENESS

*"Then said Jesus, Father, forgive them; for they know not what they do. And they parted his raiment, and cast lots." (Luke 23:34)*

One Easter Sunday after service, we arrived at a friend's home to celebrate the power our Lord's resurrection. My friend slotted in the movie *The Passion of the Christ.* As we watched the movie, it came to the part where they battered our Lord Jesus Christ, spat on Him, insulted and did all manner of injustice to Him. Then they nailed Him to the cross. At the point of giving up His life, He looked down and prayed a prayer of forgiveness, saying, "Father, forgive them, for they know not what they do" (Luke 23:34).

Stephen, as the Bible recorded, also prayed a prayer of forgiveness on behalf of those who stoned him to death under the instruction of Saul, who was later converted and known as Paul. Stephen prayed and asked God not to place a judgment to his persecutors:

Then they cast him out of the city and stoned him. And the witnesses laid down their garments at the feet of a young man named Saul. And as they were stoning Stephen, he called out, "Lord Jesus, receive my spirit."

And falling to his knees he cried out with a loud voice, "Lord, do not hold this sin against them." And when he had said this, he fell asleep. (Acts 7:58–60)

God honored this prayer, because Saul was forgiven and later became one of the most influential and most well-known, radical apostles of his day. That is the power of what a forgiveness prayer can do.

King David of the Bible is another leader who understood the power of forgiveness. Although King Saul tried to kill David, the Bible records that Saul's camp kept getting weaker and weaker, while David's camp kept getting stronger and stronger. The reason is simple: at every opportunity David had to destroy Saul, he would save Saul's life instead. That is the power of forgiveness.

That Easter Sunday I experienced a revelation that has changed my life for good. The movie *The Passion of the Christ* made it so real for me to understand more truly what forgiveness means, especially as a leader. "They do not know what they do" remains a key phrase for me. So when people offend me, I should forgive them because "they do not know what they do." Indeed, if they really knew what they were doing, they would not have done it. This happened during the season when I was going through a lot as a new immigrant, having just arrived in the United States. I had a thick accent—so thick that it impacted me in the workplace and at my local church. Unfortunately, I experienced the false support of my coworkers, who stated that they loved my accent; only later did I learn that they could not understand what I was saying and talked about me behind my back.

I had a terrible experience on my very first job here in the United States. The president and CEO of the company hired me because I opened up my heart to him about how difficult it had been for me to secure employment. He had compassion and hired me based on trust and the fact that we are both believers. I started with great enthusiasm, but within few months, my coworkers, who pretended they liked me, were the same people who framed me and brought a false witness to testify against me. My boss, a believer in Jesus, my brother in Christ, never gave me an opportunity to defend myself or counter the claims against me. The hurt I experienced was real! He decreased my work hours from five days each week to being on call. To further impact the situation, my wife was due to arrive from Nigeria soon, and I was nearing the deadline to find an apartment for us. Each time I look back, I always have a reason to thank God for the grace given to forgive my coworkers and employer. They knew they were wrong and that they hurt me. However, they did not know that God would use the experience to make me stronger and seek God more, ultimately building a more robust relationship with Him.

## Sources of Unforgiveness

During their assignments, many pastors are frequently wounded and experience situations that may challenge their hearts in the area of forgiveness. One pastor, Pastor Edward (fictitious) shared his heart with me about the hurt he experienced from a pastor he invited to minister at the church. Pastor Chucks (fictitious) had a significant impact on the congregation. The word and prophetic ministry gift of God on Pastor Chucks blessed them. Members of the congregation began going to Pastor Chucks for spiritual counseling and prayer. While Pastor Edward was aware, he had no idea of the harm done to the congregants.

One of the women in the church later told Pastor Edward how Pastor Chucks had called her on the phone and requested $1,000. She also alerted him that Pastor Chucks had done the same to several church members, collecting money before praying for them. It became evident to Pastor Edward that he had made a terrible mistake. He stepped in to stop and clean up the mess his ministry colleague had made in his church. It was too late; Pastor Chucks had already stolen the hearts of several members with his strange doctrine. Second Samuel 15:6 records, "And on this manner did Absalom to all Israel that came to the king for judgment: so Absalom stole the hearts of the men of Israel." Rather than listen to Pastor Edward, these congregants chose to continue with Pastor Chucks. As if that were not enough, Pastor Chucks opened up a fellowship in the same city, and nearly half of the congregation left Pastor Edward to follow. It was heartbreaking for Pastor Edward, considering all the labor he had done to build the church. By God's grace, however, Pastor Edward's ministry recovered! Another reminder of the need for pastors to pray for one another and for congregants to pray for their pastors.

Lead and associate pastors sometimes share this story. Many times, lead pastors have become overprotective of their congregations because of the frequent cases where associate pastors win the heart of people and leave to start new churches. In some cases, an associate pastor hears the call to pastor from God, and does all right things, yet the lead pastor will not approve and release him. When the associate decides to go, the lead pastor will never have anything to do with that associate or their ministry. Another example is when members decide to leave and join another church; pastors often hold grudges. I have witnessed many cases where the pastor never speaks a word again to the person who left. Some pastors pretend to be on good terms but, deep in their hearts, are very bitter.

Pastors appreciate members who are very dedicated to serving and are committed givers to the church. Pastors feel connected to those members who are loyal to them, those who bless them financially, and those who will run with the pastor's ideas without questioning or challenging them. Those members who invite their friends to the church and those who will never miss a program. When any of this changes, pastors are thrown off and may become hurt or bitter. Whether this is the pastor's fault for placing so much confidence in the people or the people's fault for lack of authenticity, the pastor has to be able to forgive.

## Impact of Unforgiveness

At the end of a leadership conference I once attended, some pastors began to narrate how intolerant they can be of members who are not committed and who do not support the ministry. One of the pastors actually mentioned that he doesn't answer calls from those who do not pay their tithes or serve in the local assembly. Regardless of their circumstances, some pastors do not consider individuals. The truth is, whether the pastors do it intentionally or not, we ought to love everyone without being partial. God is not a respecter of people, and pastors should not be either. We are to treat people equally. If a member offends the pastor in any situation, the pastor is obligated to forgive. It does not matter whether the member asks forgiveness or not. Jesus expects all believers to forgive. He taught forgiveness as a prerequisite for being forgiven. As we have already explained, pastors often have experiences that require forgiveness. Truthfully, there is no space for unforgiveness along the journey of completing God's assignments for our lives.

Unforgiveness dries up the anointing and gives birth to what I call spiritual cancer. The longer a pastor holds on to unforgiveness, the greater the works of the flesh manifest. Common are anger, bitterness, strife, hatred, jealousy, envy, complaining, gossiping, comparisons, and division. If we desire the power of God, we must walk in the Spirit. Walking in the Spirit makes us more spiritual than fasting and praying alone. Just as unforgiveness gives birth to the works of the flesh, which I call spiritual cancer, forgiveness gives birth to the fruits of the Spirit—namely love, joy, peace, patience,

kindness, goodness, faithfulness, gentleness, and self-control.
Now, we are walking in the Spirit, living under an open
heaven. Every pastor's wish is to have heaven open over him.
One word we hear from God makes a huge difference and can
accomplish in a short time what laboring for years on our own
cannot achieve.

## The Power of Forgiveness

Let us consider the giant heart of our Lord Jesus Christ. He
knew that Peter would deny Him, yet He prayed for him:
"And the Lord said, Simon, Simon, behold, Satan hath desired
to have you, that he may sift you as wheat: But I have prayed
for thee, that thy faith fail not: and when thou art converted,
strengthen thy brethren" (Luke 22:31–32). We are Christ followers and need to operate in the perfect example of our Lord
Jesus Christ. He understood people's personalities and worked
with them accordingly. How about Judas Iscariot? Jesus knew
that he would betray Him, yet He worked with Judas. It is
incredible to witness the heart Jesus displayed during his ministry. Having hearts like Jesus will help us do likewise during
the course of our assignments. The most amazing lesson to
learn here is not just that Jesus knew that Judas Iscariot would
betray Him—but that at the point of His betrayal, Jesus still
called Judas Iscariot a friend. Matt 26:50 records, "And Jesus
said unto him, Friend, wherefore art thou come? Then came
they, and laid hands on Jesus and took him."

Forgiveness is crucial for a fruitful ministry. It opens our
hearts to love everyone who comes our way. It also helps us to
carry out our assignment without being partial. I remember a
particular anniversary ceremony of the Men of Faith Network.
We were very short of funds to make our preparations. It
became so hard on me that I allowed bitterness to step in,
because I felt that many who truly believed in the vision and
truly understood the vision should have contributed toward
the ceremony as agreed. Funds didn't come until the very last

moment. The board decided, as a last resort, to send an urgent email to MOFN members, believing that God would touch their hearts to give. As we sent out the emails, a particular leader called and told me to check our bank account. I looked at the account and noticed a deposit that covered the deficiency, with money left over. I went home praying my heart out, asking God to bless this man.

The Holy Spirit convicted me about the feelings I had toward the board and MOFN members, regarding our being financially short. He pointed out the frustration in my heart, and how I had placed more confidence in men than in God's provision. The Holy Spirit also pointed out that I had not celebrated the men who had been laboring with me the whole time, while I did celebrate this one brother for a single monetary gift. I was partial, and it was not right. I needed to ask my colleagues' forgiveness more than offer it to them. I reconciled with the Holy Spirit right away! Truly my heart was bitter, and I had not realized that I was operating in unforgiveness until the Holy Spirit mentioned it.

The story of the prodigal son is another example of the power of forgiveness and is worth emulating as leaders. The father had every reason not to allow the son back into his house, considering all he had done. However, the Bible states that he saw his son coming from far away and had compassion: Luke 15:20, "And he arose, and came to his father. But when he was yet a great way off, his father saw him, and had compassion, and ran, and fell on his neck, and kissed him." As pastors, there are so many instances where people we trained, nurtured, and cared for have betrayed us, disappointed us, stolen the hearts of people, or were against us. May we be compassionate enough to accept them when they return. Whether or not the offender returns or repents, let our hearts be filled with the spirit of forgiveness. Let the fathers forgive their spiritual children, and let the children forgive their spiritual fathers.

Forgiveness manifests when we reach the point of praying for those who have wronged us, as Job did (Job 42:10). We might say with our lips that we have forgiven them, but honestly, the test of our faith hangs on praying for and wishing them well, from the heart.

During the course of one's assignment as a pastor, offenses are inevitable. However, we have to be more like Jesus and learn how to navigate consistently around offenses and avoid creating moments that may cause us to be offended by others. Matthew 17:24–27 is an excellent example of how Jesus was intentional about avoiding offense. A legitimate son of the soil, as a Jew, He was not supposed to pay tribute to Rome. To avoid offense, He sent Peter fishing, knowing there would be money in the mouth of a fish to pay the tribute and move forward.

Good health can also be ascribed to forgiveness. When one operates with a forgiving spirit, the mind becomes stable, allowing joy and peace to fill the heart. The heart that is filled with joy and peace has fewer chances of sickness. Proverbs 17:22 states, "A merry heart doeth good like a medicine: but a broken spirit drieth the bones." The will of God is for us to forgive one another. We should guard ourselves by forgiving people, as well as by asking others to forgive us so we can enjoy the grace of God to the fullest as we serve. When grace is at work, God orders our footsteps aright and fights our battles for us.

## Chapter 5

# THROWING IN THE TOWEL

*"Therefore now, O Lord, take, I beseech thee, my life from me; for it is better for me to die than to live." (Jonah 4:3)*

In boxing matches, when a cornerman throws the towel onto the floor of the ring, it signifies to the referee that the fighter, although struggling to stay in the fight, is in danger. The fighter has exhausted all of his mental energy and physical strength in an attempt to win the fight. The hope for the title of "Winner" is what keeps the fighter on the mat, hoping and praying for renewed energy and strength to finish the rounds. Unfortunately, by this time there seems to be no recourse except to throw in the towel. Once the referee sees the towel, he puts an end to the fight.

In this chapter, "throwing in the towel" is synonymous with committing suicide, putting an end to the fight of life. I want to be very clear that there are several positive alternatives to suicide. Choosing life may mean having difficult conversations with a spouse, children, congregation, church board, or others about our concerns. The office of pastor is one of the five ascension gifts Jesus left to prepare the saints for His returning. If God has indeed called one to this office, He has already prepared for a successful finish, even in the face of adversity and moments of defeat. Perhaps you operate in this office and have realized you are functioning in the wrong place. Thank God for grace! There is always time to hear His voice, seek the Holy Spirit, and get on the correct path. It is never too late to find your assignment and do God's will.

Many pastors consider or have considered suicide. Jonah struggled with completing the assignment God ordained for him; he asked that his life be taken. Elijah, too, ran for his life, wanting to throw in the towel. Honestly speaking, this chapter is probably the most important reason why I wrote this book. We need to pray for pastors and their families more intensely because they come against such diverse challenges in their day-to-day duties. Many are suffering and are dying silently without letting anyone know about it.

While attending a leadership conference in Aba, Nigeria, in March 2016, I was asked to pray for the leaders. The Lord laid it upon my heart to pray for someone who had been contemplating quitting the ministry. I gave the word and prayed for this person. After the ministration, a woman walked up to the podium and announced that she was the one the Lord had singled out. She said she was not just planning to quit the ministry, but she was about to take her own life. We later learned that this lady, an evangelist, was also a widow. She had so much going against her in her life. She was struggling to feed her children. Her ministry was not flourishing. Preaching had become more difficult than before. Thankfully, her son had shared with her the flyer for the service I attended and, in fact, actively encouraged her to attend. She attended, she thought, to appease her son, not realizing God already had a plan!

A well-known organization that helps pastors and Christians facing persecution globally lost their former president to suicide. He was having an adulterous affair. Rather than face the shame, he took his life. Another unfortunate example happened near Hazel Crest, Illinois. A pastor shot and killed himself after his wife's death. He had previously made claims of continually hearing her voice.

Many pastors all over the world are giving in to suicide for one reason or another. Discouragement can be the inspiration for many deeper issues such as burnout, depression, fornication, adultery, money laundering, or divorce.

Statistics from www.PastorBurnout.com and the *New York Times* (August 1, 2010):

Members of the clergy now suffer from obesity, hypertension, and depression at rates higher than most Americans. In the last decade, their use of antidepressants has risen, while their life expectancy has fallen. Many would change jobs if they could.

- 13 percent of active pastors are divorced.
- 23 percent have been fired or pressured to resign at least once in their careers.
- 25 percent don't know where to turn when they have a family or personal conflict or issue.
- 25 percent of pastors' wives see their husband's work schedule as a source of conflict.
- 33 percent felt burned out within their first five years of ministry.
- 33 percent say that being in ministry is an outright hazard to their family.
- 40 percent of pastors and 47 percent of spouses are suffering from burnout, frantic schedules, and/or unrealistic expectations.
- 45 percent of pastors' wives say the greatest danger to them and their family is physical, emotional, mental, and spiritual burnout.
- 45 percent of pastors say that they've experienced depression or burnout to the extent that they needed to take a leave of absence from ministry.
- 50 percent feel unable to meet the needs of the job.

- 52 percent of pastors say they and their spouses believe that being in pastoral ministry is hazardous to their family's well-being and health.
- 56 percent of pastors' wives say that they have no close friends.
- 57 percent would leave the pastorate if they had somewhere else to go or some other vocation they could do.
- 70 percent don't have any close friends.
- 75 percent report severe stress—causing anguish, worry, bewilderment, anger, depression, fear, and alienation.
- 80 percent of pastors say they have insufficient time with their spouse.
- 80 percent believe that pastoral ministry affects their families negatively.
- 90 percent feel unqualified or poorly prepared for ministry.
- 90 percent work more than 50 hours a week.
- 94 percent feel under pressure to have a perfect family.
- 1,500 pastors leave their ministries each month due to burnout, conflict, or moral failure.
- Doctors, lawyers, and clergy have the most problems with drug abuse, alcoholism, and suicide.

These statistics bring to light things pastors have to contend with on a regular basis while living out their commitment to the call of God on their lives. Unfortunately, these concerns go unnoticed and improperly addressed. Worse, many pastors resolve the impact of these issues by walking away from ministry, their families, or their very lives. Consider the following areas in which pastors contend.

## Profession or Calling

Calling and profession are not the same; there is a difference. A calling is an unction that pulls toward a particular area or group of people. It is a consistent pulling on the mind and heart. A profession is something one studies and receives training for, generally with the expectation of compensation. A calling requires God's grace. A profession requires desire and study. It is critical to ask ourselves whether, in our own lives, pastoring is a calling from God or a profession chosen for its misleading attractiveness.

Jonah went astray, trying to avoid his calling. God gave Jonah a specific task. Although he did not want to complete the task, Jonah found it impossible to run from God. The Bible records that God prepared a unique fish, which swallowed Jonah to get his attention. Jonah soon realized that he could not run from his God-given assignment.

There is always an unusual grace that accompanies our calling. It is this grace that Jonah experienced as God reminded him of his calling. We should be encouraged in our calling to know that God sees the end from the beginning, and will always release the grace that will see us through. Entering ministry should not be looked at as a career or profession with ambition. Once called into ministry, it is possible or likely that it becomes one's profession by default. We have to realize the importance of seeking God for direction regarding our calling. Upon understanding and accepting our calling, we then have to commit to the process and please God. 2 Peter 1:10 states, "Therefore, brothers, be all the more diligent to confirm your calling and election, for if you practice these qualities you will never fall."

## Understanding of the Vision

Many are genuinely called of God but lack understanding of God's vision for the call. For example, someone called to be an evangelist who becomes a pastor risks becoming frustrated because the grace of each office is not the same. The grace that accompanies the evangelist's assignment will not necessarily function or be sufficient to carry out the pastoral assignment.

When I received the call of God to be an evangelist, I had a clear understanding, by His grace, that it was not a call to be a pastor. As the founding president of Men of Faith Network, I understand the role of a pastor. I oversee leaders and the regular functions of the ministry. However, I am aware of my calling, and it is not to the office of the pastor or to lead a congregation.

For some, throwing in the towel is due to lack of sufficiently understanding their calling. When God asked Jeremiah what he saw, Jeremiah saw clearly, and God responded that he saw well. Jeremiah did not just see a tree; he saw an almond tree. He was very specific and clear about what he saw. Many see their calling into ministry but lack the understanding to see precisely where they belong. When we identify where we belong, the Lord performs. He is the one that gives the vision, and He will make all provision. Except the Lord builds, the laborers build in vain. Ministry should be served with passion and joy-filled hearts, seeing God performing His work through us. Jeremiah 1:11–12 records, "Moreover the word of the Lord came unto me, saying, Jeremiah, what seest thou? And I said, I see a rod of an almond tree. Then said the Lord unto me, Thou hast well seen: for I will hasten my word to perform it."

## Sin

Acknowledging our areas of weakness in ministry will help us beyond measure. Before salvation, I was in sexual bondage. Now as a believer and a minister, I would be unwise to ignore this as I move forward in ministry. While this is no longer a battle, I have to acknowledge it as an area the enemy, or my flesh, may present as temptation. I am careful not to engage in ministry, prayer, or counseling alone with women. Paul said that those things he would like to do, he found himself not doing them, but the things he did not want to do are the very things he found himself doing. He concluded by saying that it was no longer himself but the sin that lives in him. We need to resist sin by all means, no matter how little or big it is. Sin is sin. I once heard a preacher say, "You should not say, 'I can't be tempted to steal any money that does not belong to me' until you find yourself alone with money that does not belong to you." When one overcomes a grave temptation, he can then testify. We should strive always to be holy because God is holy and expects us to be holy: "But as he which hath called you is holy, so be ye holy in all manner of conversation; because it is written, Be ye holy; for I am holy" (1 Peter 1:15–16).

## Repentance

Sin often brings with it condemnation and guilt. To fall or sin is one thing, but it is altogether different to remain fallen or in sin. Staying down allows the sin to tighten its grip, making it more difficult to address and repent, and could potentially lead us closer to throwing in the towel. God requires repentance when we err. Peter betrayed Jesus. Judas betrayed Him as well. The difference was that Peter became remorseful of his sin, repented, and moved forward to become the archbishop among the apostles, who did great works. Judas, however, had remorse over his sin but remained in it and chose suicide. This is precisely the phenomenon we see today. No matter what the sin is, all God needs is genuine repentance, not remorse. It does not matter what people say. Our focus should be on what God is saying. He has the final say! When God forgives, we need to accept it and forgive ourselves. It does not matter if people never forgive. Let us not allow pride or shame to deprive us of genuine repentance. David was a man in the Bible who understood the importance of acknowledging his sin and genuinely repenting:

> Have mercy upon me, O God, according to thy lovingkindness: according unto the multitude of thy tender mercies blot out my transgressions. Wash

me throughly from mine iniquity, and cleanse me
from my sin. For I acknowledge my transgressions:
and my sin is ever before me. (Psalm 51:1–3)

## Isolation

Isolation is very common among pastors and may be one
reason suicide continues to increase among them. Pastors can
be very secretive and not allow others to learn their personal
business. Every pastor should be accountable to someone to
avoid the pressures of secrets and to help prevent them from
throwing in the towel. Most times, living and operating in
isolation and without being accountable to anyone is how false
pride enters. Leaders are genuinely deceived to feel a sense of
accomplishment when operating in false pride, thinking they
are always right, talking all the time and being unwilling to
listen to others: "A fool hath no delight in understanding, but
that his heart may discover itself" (Proverbs 18:2).

Pastors should participate in organizations that will help
them, spiritually and otherwise. Leadership conferences are
essential for pastors to attend. No pastor should achieve a
level where they feel it is no longer necessary to connect
with others. Pastors should fellowship with other ministers,
stripping off their titles so they can worship God in spirit and
truth. Pastors should be willing to open up to one another and
request personal prayers. Pastors' issues are likely to diminish
by having a prayer partner as well as an accountability partner.

Hebrews 10:25 states, "Not forsaking the assembling of
ourselves together, as the manner of some is; but exhort-
ing one another: and so much the more, as ye see the day
approaching." We often use this scripture to encourage people about the importance of membership in a local church.
However, we neglect to note that this scripture speaks to
pastors as well. Pastors should not forsake the assembly of like-
minded leaders. It is a platform for them to have the freedom

to relate to fellow ministers, share their burdens, and receive prayer. Unfortunately, many isolate themselves, giving various excuses not to fellowship with fellow ministers.

## Divorce

Divorce is another silent killer. Some divorce cases are the result of poor choice in spouses. Can two walk together except they agree? Divorce should not be the way out of a marriage that was never meant to be. Unfortunately, people enter marriage with divorce in mind as a way out if things do not go according to plan. Recently, a young pastor's death was linked to his divorce. His wife left, abandoning the family. To add to this, she was seen to be flirting around and dating other men in the same city where the pastor preached. He never recovered from the divorce. He became depressed and just let himself go. Illness eventually got the best of him. Unfortunately, he died, not having moved beyond his divorce.

I strongly encourage single pastors interested in marriage to be very careful and prayerful about whom to marry. Look for the signs God shows you, and please, do not pretend they are not there. Before I married my wife, I was in another relationship that didn't work out. We were engaged to be married. Today I am ever grateful to God. One of the signs for me was having to remind her to attend church. Our communication around ministry led to many arguments. We could never seem to get on the same page. God even showed me signs in my dreams. When I noticed that, I didn't need a prophet to help me understand. I recognized that things would not likely change after marriage, and could negatively impact me and my calling. By God's grace, I found the wife He designed for me, as evidenced by the favor upon my life.

To pastors who are already married and have concerns that you married the wrong person, you have no option but to pray and believe God to change your spouse's heart and bring the two of you into oneness. Divorce is not an option; stay in the ring! We need to fight more often on our knees and ask God for wisdom and grace to endure. Job's wife asked him to curse God and die, but Job kept his integrity; "Then said his wife unto him, Dost thou still retain thine integrity? Curse God, and die" (Job 2:9). We have to exhaust all options to keep our marriages healthy, rather than choose divorce.

Obstacles should never be a reason for divorce. Sometimes the pain caused by challenges, obstacles, or experiences may be very severe but can have a positive impact on our ministries. Ministering from the "winner's seat" is a testimony of overcoming in our own lives. Our testimonies bring passion and witness as we minister to others, making us relevant sources for them. With God, all things are possible. We need to commit every issue of our marital differences to God in prayer. God is still in the business of answering prayers. God hates divorce; it doesn't speak well of the gospel we preach. I always encourage pastors to remember three things about divorce: it brings shame to the kingdom, it brings pain to the children, and it is a silent killer of the soul.

## Death

The death of a loved one or someone close brings a great deal of pain. Everyone does not respond well to death. Death is inevitable and is sometimes a harsh truth we shy away from. However, it has been defeated, because as believers we have eternal life! 1 Corinthian 15:26 states, "The last enemy that shall be destroyed is death." Let not even the death of our loved ones separate our love from God. It is indeed a terrible thing when it happens. It is such a question that no one can answer until we meet God. Oral Roberts explained how emotionally distraught he and his wife became when they lost their daughter and son-in-law in a plane crash. He overcame by confessing the truth to himself. Eventually, God started using him and his wife to console others who had lost loved ones. Many pastors have lost loved ones, including spouses.

Keep the fires at the altar burning by declaring the word of God that sustains when we find ourselves in such a situation. God does not use death to provoke us to throw in the towel. If for anything, it is to pull us closer to Him. Although we grieve—and it is acceptable to grieve—God has a way of comforting us. Romans 8:35–39 helps us with these words:

> Who shall separate us from the love of Christ? Shall tribulation, or distress, or persecution, or famine, or nakedness, or peril, or sword? As it is written, For thy sake we are killed all the day long; we are accounted as sheep for the slaughter. Nay, in all these things we are more than conquerors through him that loved us. For I am persuaded, that neither death, nor life, nor angels, nor principalities, nor powers, nor things present, nor things to come, Nor height, nor depth, nor any other creature, shall be able to separate us from the love of God, which is in Christ Jesus our Lord.

Let's revisit the fighter from our introduction and rewrite his ending, assuming he had one last conversation with his trainer. What could that conversation have been? What could the fighter have asked his trainer? What could the trainer have instructed the fighter to do? There have been several boxing matches where the apparent loser, who had exhausted all energy and strength, found a source of revival and rejuvenation from a place deep within. Where is that place for us? As believers, that place is where our spirit communes with the Holy Spirit, who has been interceding for us the entire time. It is the place we feel the power and presence of God, and receive supernatural stamina to get back into the fight. As we get back into the fight, the power of God is all we need to attain the title of winner.

Pastor, you have to know that God's promise to you is that He will never leave you and that all things work together for good—your good—because you are called according to His purpose! Don't give up, pastor! Don't throw in the towel! There is renewed strength and vigor waiting for you in the presence of God. There, your joy is filled, your peace is increased, your vision is clear, and you are refocused on your assignment.

## Chapter 6

# REJECTION

*"But today you have rejected your God, who saves you from all your calamities and your distresses, and you have said to him, 'Set a king over us.' Now therefore present yourselves before the Lord by your tribes and by your thousands." (1 Samuel 10:19)*

A friend and mentor of mine once invited me for a one-on-one meeting. I was so excited and very much looked forward to the day. We were meeting to discuss his feedback on this book's manuscript. I yearned for his input, because he is a man filled with excellent wisdom. I genuinely liked and trusted him upon our very first contact. Our kingdom friendship has brought us together on several occasions, including in the Men of Faith Network, where he gave an outstanding message.

While I anxiously looked forward to the forthcoming meeting, I was filled with expectation. Could it be he was going to endorse the book? Was he going to connect me to great publishers? Maybe he would either sponsor the publishing or connect me to a sponsor because of his high profile in our area. My expectations were too high! I had been praying and believing God for something spectacular to happen so I could be assured that His hand was upon my writing this book. I was so desperate for encouragement and affirmation that I began to celebrate before the much-awaited meeting day.

After much anticipation, Saturday, August 12, 2017, arrived—7:00 a.m., prompt! I couldn't sleep the previous night because I had to embark on a 40- to 45-minute drive, depending on traffic. Of course, I arrived early, and as I said, my friend is a man of integrity, so he was already there waiting for me. In our usual manner, we ordered coffee, chatted for a bit, then dove directly into the goal of our meeting.

My friend and mentor looked me straight in the eyes and boldly informed me that he would not read the manuscript I had sent him because he felt our relationship was not developed enough for him to endorse my book. He went on, explaining how it was too soon for him to help. I felt rejected and despised but held my peace as he spoke. All my high expectations crashed just like an aircraft crashing down from the sky. However, as I listened, I began to relate to all his explanations of why he felt he must turn down my request. I did send the manuscript to so many other pastors and leaders, who did not even bother to respond. He at least responded, and we barely knew each other. I began to reason with him, and indeed he was right. I apologized for the task I had asked of him and affirmed that I accepted his explanation. He was relieved and also confessed that he had found it difficult responding to me via email but wanted a face-to-face meeting so I would not misinterpret his response. I did appreciate his boldness in telling me the truth, which others who did not respond could not tell me. We prayed and parted for the day.

The ride home was drastically different from the ride to our meeting! I had left my home with high expectations and was returning with no astonishing news to share with my wife. As I drove, my peace dissipated; I felt totally let down. I thought it would have been better for me if he had responded via email or a chat over the phone. I was just overwhelmed as I drove home. When I arrived home, I turned on my gadget, checked for messages, and—WOW! The Lord is a God of comfort. Another pastor, whom I had not met face-to-face, had reviewed the manuscript, endorsed it on her church letterhead, and stated that

I should not feel like a stranger! She even offered more help if I needed her. Amazing, isn't it? There I was, from rejected and deflated a few hours earlier, to accepted with wide open arms and support. There was nothing left to do but praise God who knows how best to keep us focused, even at a time of rejection.

When these two incidents happened, I learned that personalities can be instrumental to rejection. Personalities affect people's decisions. I see my mentor more as an introvert. He's very reserved and prefers a selected few around him. On the other hand, though I had not met the other pastor in person, I could tell by her letter that she is an extrovert. We need to understand that personality can influence people's decisions.

Another cause of rejection may be connected with personal qualifications. Imagine a pastor needing to hire an accountant who chooses to hire a church member based on their explanation of experience in the area. After working with the new accountant for a few months, the pastor realizes that he did not make the best decision. As much as he would like to retain the parishioner, likely for personal reasons, the pastor realizes that he must act in the best interest of the church. An obvious, seemingly easy move for the pastor, but perhaps an emotional experience for the parishioner, possibly connected to rejection.

I published my first book, *Can I Take a Little Wine*, in 2009. My book never sold beyond my friends and family members. I was so sure the book had great content. But the writing style was very poor. I wrestled rejection because the book did not do well. I felt people did not respect my work and that I that I did not have enough popularity to be a best-selling author. In hindsight, I am happy it never sold, because looking back now, it's a horrible read. If my book is horrible to me, how do I expect others to read it or invest their money for it? I lacked knowledge of advance writing and editing, and I never thought to hire help. In an effort to cut costs, I did not allow critics to review the book before publishing. Clearly, *Who Prays for the Pastor* will sell far more copies because I have invested in the right areas!

As believers, it is important for us to fully understand the assignments God places upon us. There are seasons or moments in a pastor or leader's life when things just feel right. There is an anointing attached to each call that enables the grace one needs in order to successfully complete the assignments God has called us to. Many times we are passionate about doing something—but is that really the will of God? I am sure there are many pastors who will admit to having "missed it" and felt rejected. As I mentioned earlier, an evangelist operating as a pastor is likely to face rejection by the congregation due to an inability and lack of grace to function as a pastor.

In the Bible, we see that David was passionate about building a temple for God—yet he experienced rejection. God told him that his son Solomon would build the temple, not David. We have to be careful to discern the difference between desire or zeal and the will of God. Much time can be wasted chasing desire and not the Father's plan for us. Praying for pastors is a must when it comes to knowing the will of God. There is nothing more disappointing to a pastor and congregation than feeling rejected by God because He doesn't anoint or prosper their plans. Proverbs 19:21 helps us: "Many are the plans in the mind of a man, but it is the purpose of the Lord that will stand." While Paul teaches us that all things work together for our good, God absolutely wants us to know and follow His plans for our lives. Pray that pastors will be more passionate about God's will than their own plans.

Habakkuk 2:2 records, "And the Lord answered me: 'Write the vision; make it plain on tablets, so he may run who reads it. For still the vision awaits its appointed time; it hastens to the end—it will not lie. If it seems slow, wait for it; it will surely come; it will not delay.'" Moses, at a later age in his life, found out that he had been called to deliver the Israelites from Egypt. He instantly began operating in his own timing. He met rejection, not because he was out of God's calling, but because he did not wait for God. I don't know how many of us have fallen into such situations. If we are to avoid rejection, we should write the vision as we receive it and wait for the appointed time. This is where seeking God is important. Congregations are far more likely to push vision when they recognize God's timing for it. The opposite, rejection, occurs when they discern that pastors have missed God. Are we praying for pastors?

Although we do not like rejection, any of us can testify to numerous times we have experienced it. If God, the Creator, can face rejection from His children, how much more can we? "But today you have rejected your God, who saves you from all your calamities and your distresses, and you have said to him, 'Set a king over us.' Now therefore present yourselves before the Lord by your tribes and by your thousands" (1 Samuel 10:19).

There is a degree to which we must accept rejection as leaders. It is important for pastors to understand how to put rejection in proper perspective. As it was with Saul, the same is true for pastors after God's own heart. Saul was God's chosen first king over the children of Israel. Note that Samuel pointed out to the Israelites how they rejected God as their ultimate Father and King, to ask for a more relatable, human king. If God was so rejected, why would He accept His people's rejection and honor their request? Was it because He's sovereign? Was it because He's all-knowing, having already seen their future? Notice that, at the root of Israel's rejecting God was the truth of their heart as a people. Pastors, in some matters people are rejecting the Father, not you. In other matters God may allow you to experience it because He has different plans for you.

Every pastor or minister who answers the Lord's calling will surely be rejected by some people. Not everyone who starts a ministry will immediately have many followers. Some people want to associate themselves with established churches rather than churches that are just beginning. For those who are about to be ordained or moving into ministry, bear in mind that you will be despised and rejected by few. Note that Saul was despised and some the people of Israel said, "How can this man save us?" They even brought no gifts to honor him (1 Samuel 10:27). Obviously Saul was belittled, but the Bible records that King Saul held his peace. Learn this approach from the scripture and never take offense with anybody. Holding your peace is vital at moments of rejection. Every great pastor has a story to tell of how he or she was despised and rejected at the start of their ministerial journey. Either way, just as Saul held his peace, we ought to learn to do the same in order to enhance and advance in our callings. Some will reject you, and many others will accept you.

Congregants, pray for your pastors as they navigate the waters of ministry. Yes, our pastors will not always make the best decisions, much like we at times make poor choices. Our role is to allow pastors space to be human, to support the visions God gives them, to work diligently alongside them, and to intercede for them along the way. Understand that rejection is not limited to church or ministry-related issues. While there are those who hail pastors and ministry leaders as supernatural beings, the truth is, they are not! Pastors and leaders may carry personal hurts connected to rejection that date back as far as their childhood. They need prayer for inner healing and deliverance, just as we parishioners do. When you view your pastors, see them as people, anointed by God with a supernatural grace to carry out the assignments on their lives. When we put Hebrews 4:15 in perspective, I believe we will have the right understanding about our pastors: "For we have not an high priest which cannot be touched with the feeling of our infirmities; but was in all points tempted like as we are, yet without sin." Now, I don't include this verse to suggest that pastors are without sin. However, I include it to emphasize that Jesus, our Savior and Lord, experienced our infirmities. Naturally our pastors do as well. Are you praying for your pastor?

## Chapter 7
# SPIRITUAL GIFTS

*"Pursue love, and earnestly desire the spiritual gifts,
especially that you may prophesy." (1 Corinthians 14:1)*

There seems to be confusion in the church as to what the
gifts of the Spirit are and how they were given to benefit the
Body. In 1 Corinthians 12:8–10, the Apostle Paul lists nine
gifts of the Spirit: word of wisdom, word of knowledge,
discerning of spirits, diversity of tongues, interpretation of
tongues, prophecy, faith, healing, and working of miracles.
He explains that these gifts are to unify the Body of Christ,
the Church, to mobilize her to advance the Kingdom. Any
other use of these gifts, especially for personal gain, is a perversion. A paraphrased definition of perversion is deliberate
distortion or corruption of original intent, often without
regard to consequences.

Signs and wonders move people, tempting many to pursue
spiritual gifts without proper understanding and revelation,
generally resulting in occults and false representations of God's
word. Many pastors have fallen prey innocently, while some
have sought it deliberately. The kingdom of darkness exists
and still operates today with demonic perversions of spiritual
gifts. Satan wants to build his kingdom too, recruiting even
the very elect. There are many pastors with genuine spiritual

gifts who abuse or pervert them to suit their agendas. More are using their spiritual gifts out of selfish ambition rather than proclaiming Christ out of love.

Two biblical examples of this were experienced by Moses and Daniel. When God sent Moses and Aaron to Pharaoh, Aaron's staff turned into a serpent and Pharaoh's magicians did the same:

> Then the Lord said to Moses and Aaron, "When Pharaoh says to you, 'Prove yourselves by working a miracle,' then you shall say to Aaron, 'Take your staff and cast it down before Pharaoh, that it may become a serpent.'" So Moses and Aaron went to Pharaoh and did just as the Lord commanded. Aaron cast down his staff before Pharaoh and his servants, and it became a serpent. Then Pharaoh summoned the wise men and the sorcerers, and they, the magicians of Egypt, did the same by their secret arts. (Exodus 7:8–11)

The same thing happened with Daniel when interpreting the king's dreams. King Nebuchadnezzar did not understand his dreams and would call upon astrologers for interpretations. When they failed, he became aware of God's gifting in Daniel's life. Daniel was able to accurately interpret the king's dream, finding favor with the king.

The goal of this chapter is to uncover the lack of understanding and misuse of spiritual gifts and bring attention to the fact that many false prophets are scattered all over the Body of Christ. Matthew 24:11 records, "And many false prophets will arise and lead many astray." In many parts of the world today, sorcerers, magicians, occultists, and those practicing voodoo, to mention only a few, are all operating ministries with "spiritual gifts," deceiving as many as they can, including desperate pastors. There is no error or deed God is not able to forgive if we sincerely repent. Pray for pastors who have fallen into this trap, that they will repent, be delivered, and become faithful servants of God.

For pastors, properly understanding and operating in the spiritual gifts is essential for fruitful ministry. These gifts are evidence of the Holy Spirit's presence in the lives of believers as well as in the local church. When pastors and congregants develop awareness and understanding of the gifts of the Spirit, there will be a spiritual balance within the local church. Although I am writing in the context of pastors, know that the gifts of the Spirit are not limited to pastors; they are given by the Spirit regardless of position or title. Spiritual gifts are for believers. Paul writes that one should earnestly desire spiritual gifts—while pursuing love (1 Corinthians 14:1). Note that in 1 Corinthians 13, Paul teaches that love is more important than any gift or supernatural ability. Love does not result in perversion. The more pastors lead from a place of love, and rightly function in spiritual gifts, the more followers will respond from a place of love and operate in spiritual gifts.

The love of a pastor does not allow others to pollute the gifts of the Spirit to manipulate those whom God has placed under his care. Pastors shepherd the flock of God. Shepherds are protective and desire only the best for their flock. Pastors, ask the Holy Spirit to teach you how to love as the Father loves. Congregants, pray for pastors, that they will operate in the gifts of the Spirit from a place of love.

Love is one of the fruits of the Spirit, which are essential to attain heaven. Just as spiritual gifts are vital for cohesive ministry here on earth, fruits of the Spirit are designed to build godly character that enhances the ministry of the Spirit. We often focus much more on the spiritual gifts than the fruits of the Spirit. Clearly, both are necessary if the Father provides them. There does have to be balance. Spiritual gifts are great, but when the fruits of the Spirit are evident in our lives, individuals (believers and nonbelievers) are more receptive to the anointing that operates through the gifts of the Spirit: "But the fruit of the Spirit is love, joy, peace, patience, kindness, goodness, faithfulness, gentleness, self-control; against such things there is no law" (Galatians 5:22–23). Pastors need to know that their followers love them—not based upon gifts and empty words, but from hearts of committed people dedicated to the vision of their leaders. John 15:13 records, "Greater love has no one than this that someone lay down his life for his friends." God uses the fruits of Spirit to drive the gifts of the Spirit.

Pastors, please do run with the gifts and fruits of the Spirit, but do not forget the goal of Christian living and ministry: making disciples and preparing for Christ's return. Pastors, like us laity, have to pursue the assignments God has given each of us. Permit me to paraphrase Jesus in Mark 8—"What shall it profit a pastor to use spiritual gifts leading people to heaven and miss heaven himself?" We must ask ourselves, "What shall it profit a pastor to use spiritual gifts to obtain material needs and miss heaven himself?" Consider heaven today as you read this book. Jesus is coming. When? I do not know, but one thing is for sure: Jesus is coming. Do not get me wrong; we need all the spiritual gifts for ministry. However, we must discipline ourselves every day in pursuit of the fruits of the Spirit. Paul writes, "But I discipline my body and keep it under control, lest after preaching to others I myself should be disqualified" (1 Corinthians 9:27).

Two kingdoms are in existence, and they are the kingdom of darkness and the kingdom of light. We should understand, but not become consumed by, the gifts of the Spirit. Otherwise, we innocently will keep working for the kingdom of darkness on the assumption that we are working for the kingdom of light. It is possible to miss heaven with the gift of the Spirit, but it's not possible to miss heaven with the fruit of the Spirit. Matthew 7:21–23 records,

> "Not everyone who says to me, 'Lord, Lord,' will enter the kingdom of heaven, but the one who does the

will of my Father who is in heaven. On that day many will say to me, 'Lord, Lord, did we not prophesy in your name, and cast out demons in your name, and do many mighty works in your name?' And then will I declare to them, 'I never knew you; depart from me, you workers of lawlessness.'"

For congregants, here comes the question again, "Who prays for the pastor?" All you have read in this chapter is to open your eyes to the importance of praying for your pastor. Your pastor is just as human as you are. Most often, pastors fall into traps unknowingly. God is not the author of confusion and division. His desire is that there be oneness in the Body of Christ.

Hebrews 13:17 encourages us to "obey your leaders and submit to them, for they are keeping watch over your souls, as those who will have to give an account. Let them do this with joy and not with groaning, for that would be of no advantage to you." This passage speaks of the humility of both pastors and laity. Pastors are to remain humble before the Lord in order to receive revelation and understanding of the souls entrusted them by God. Laity have to remain humble enough to recognize that our pastors are given by God, from His heart, to help us. Pray for your pastor. God is holding him accountable to pray for you.

## Chapter 8

# FINANCIAL PRESSURE

The high cost of debt in ministry is increasing drastically. According to a research article published by www.stewardshipcentral.org, about 73 percent of American churches are in debt. Seventy-three percent! The average debt load for those churches is north of $4 million—and that's just the *average*. The largest churches carry an average of more than $15 million in debt, with the highest at $28 million dollars.

Now, if the average churches or ministries are struggling with debt, that tells you why the kingdom of God is not progressing as it should or dominating in financial strength the way it should. Bear in mind that the burden of financial strain in ministries today is linked to pastors. That's why if a ministry is in debt, the pastor is under serious financial pressure. The first person to be notified either by church leaders or collection agencies about unpaid bills is the pastor. Most developing countries do not have organized lending agents or banks that can loan money the way it is in developed countries like the United States. So what happens in these developing countries is that lack of funds literally has shut down some churches. Some of the pastors, as a last choice, resort to borrowing money from their church members to balance church expenses. When paying back the loan is not met as agreed, conflicts set in with the members. Sadder still, some pastors even compromise their faith so they can get financial support from their affluent church members. In return, such contributors screen the pastor's sermons for personal reasons. The pressure in this is that a breach would likely result in loss of more funds.

I remember a pastor once shared that the Sunday offering and tithe collected was not even enough to pay for the renting space for the church. Another shared how the church's power was shut off and they could not have regular services. Most often, these pastors may be faced with financial pressures they never signed up for. When pastors are faced with financial pressure, it challenges their peace of mind and their ability to lead effectively and properly attend to the ministry needs of their congregations. What a huge task! In addition to the financial struggles of the church, many pastors also experience personal financial strains. Some struggle to make ends meet and provide basic needs for their families before even attempting to bail the church out. Successfully working through these financial difficulties often causes pastors to feel entitlement or more ownership of the physical church because of their sacrifices and pressures. Pastors certainly need prayer in the area of finance, as it has the capacity to overwhelm them to the point of burnout, ineffective ministry practices, or worse, completely walking away from the church.

Operating with a budget should reduce financial pressures, but many times pastors operate without a budget and call it faith. However, the Bible teaches us, "For which of you, desiring to build a tower, does not first sit down and count the cost, whether he has enough to complete it? Otherwise, when he has laid a foundation and is not able to finish, all who see it begin to mock him, saying, 'This man began to build and was not able to finish'" (Luke 14:28–30). Jesus Himself taught the disciples about financial discipline. Pastors need to carry out assignments with a budget and be accountable to their financial team for handling the business side of the ministry. These are ideal stewardship practices.

Knowingly or unknowingly, pastors drift from enriching members' lives spiritually to focusing on the business of the church. At times they neglect the primary goal of winning souls and raising disciples. Sometimes teachings are more secular than spiritual. With so much emphasis on financial solutions, attention to members diminishes. Fortunately, there are those pastors who have survived financial storms presented by ministry and the church. Their victory propels them to teach more on financial balance and planning. While sharing the wisdom of overcoming financial struggles with congregation is important, it should not become the focus of a pastor's sermons. The Gospel message and living lives of breakthrough should continue to be the main target of regular ministry.

Pastors should experience routine self-evaluations to examine their work in light of God's vision for the church. Many agenda items pastors embark upon may be selfish or simply off-target. This has potential to bring unnecessary financial pressure upon them as well as the congregation. Instead, if pastors focus on God's agenda, they will be graced for any accompanying pressure. I shared in a previous chapter about not meeting a set target for fundraising during the Men of Faith Network's anniversary. Indeed, the primary reason for celebrating is to appreciate God, who keeps sustaining the vision. But after going through that financial pressure in our fifth year, I had to re-evaluate my faith and realized I had missed something somewhere. Second Corinthians 13:5 tells us, "Examine yourselves, whether ye be in the faith; prove your own selves. Know ye not your own selves, how that Jesus Christ is in you, except ye be reprobates?" At the Men of Faith Network's very first anniversary, it was so evident that the hand of the Lord was with us. Within three months of the thought to celebrate the first anniversary of the vision, all funds were more than enough for the event. But with subsequent celebrations, even though preparations started earlier, we struggled raising funds. The fifth year was the hardest and the most expensive. The Lord opened my eyes to see how most times we carry out programs that He didn't ask us to or that He has no interest in. God is not an author of confusion. When He gives a vision, He makes a provision. Immediately I caught this revelation, and the board agreed not to have any future anniversary celebrations. Since then, we have been progressing without any financial pressure due to anniversary programs.

Not only do unnecessary programs absorb a church's finances, but costly projects such as building or equipment purchases may place undue financial strains. Understand that ministry usually requires a physical space to worship, fellowship, and pursue God's vision. I am not saying that pastors and congregations should not make these types of purchases; I am simply saying that prayer and wisdom must be primary in the process. If a church's budget cannot handle a million-dollar property and the expenses that come with it, then it would be irresponsible of a pastor and board to pursue such a project. Seeking God from the beginning is more likely to provide the mental, emotional, and financial comfort and stability the leadership and congregation will need in order to continue progressing. This is not to negate faith in the process of purchasing high-priced things for ministry, but to encourage the wisdom and financial responsibility needed to sustain God's vision. While James says, "Faith apart from works is useless," our works should be well planned and executed.

As pastors focus on God-inspired visions with fidelity, God has a way of moving upon the hearts of people and systems in order to use us to bring His visions to pass. One pastor shared an amazing testimony of how God provided a debt-free facility to accommodate their worship services as well as an amazing program the pastor had initiated. This pastor had great passion for homeless and troubled children. He has taken several of them from the streets, allowed them into his home, and impacted their lives in awesome ways. Some of those children have become pastors themselves; others have become educated and hold good jobs or have taken up the same passion because their own lives were transformed.

This pastor's consistency and perseverance caught the eye of a stranger, who noticed the great work and was moved by God to bless the pastor's efforts. This person approached the pastor and gave him a blank check to invest in his work for God. The timing was perfect, and they were able to make a cash purchase and expand the ministry. I believe that when we are focused on our God-given vision, He will surely make a way for us, and the mission will be accomplished with ease and without financial pressure.

Recognizing that every pastor may not catch the eye of a stranger to fund their projects, having a clear understanding of financial planning and debt management is crucial for pastors, leaders, and laity alike. I strongly recommend that pastors do everything possible to bring churches out of debt or avoid incurring unnecessary debt. Avoiding debt is a sure way to overcome financial pressure. Pastors would do well to learn and understand more about financial planning and money management. There are several resources available to educate leaders on debt-free living. These lessons apply to the pastor personally, as well as to the ministry.

The issues identified in this chapter go beyond just praying for pastors. They also require things that should be done to get it right. My prayer is for God to open the eyes of pastors to debt freedom and pursue it, rather than becoming acquainted with debt and financial pressure. Falling into a mess is not the problem, but making no effort to jump out of the mess is a big problem. The greatest disaster is this: as long as a pastor is in debt and doing nothing about it, it is very possible that he will run the church into debt, and the followers will be in debt, and the grueling cycle of financial pressure and bondage to debt continues.

★★★

*The following section was contributed by Dr. Godfrey Ekhomu,*
*certified public accountant, on overcoming financial pressure.*

Understanding the impact of financial pressure is a solid prerequisite of solving the problem of financial pressure. Unneeded
financial pressure creates stress that distracts the pastor from
his original calling or mandate. The modern pastor or church
actually is not alone in this struggle. In the early church (Acts
6), the apostles had to elect deacons to manage the activities of
the church. It is important to know that the apostles themselves
asked to be excused from the day-to-day administrative functions of the church in order to focus on prayer and preaching.
Continuing in the mundane activities of the church would have
created a major distraction for the apostles in their mission. By
yielding the administrative activities to men of good report and
full of the Holy Ghost—the deacons—the apostles laid their
trust in God fully. I believe all their needs were met, with nothing lacking—all to the glory of the Lord. Briefly, based on my
profession as a certified public accountant, I have been blessed
to counsel several clients who engage in for-profit business and/
or nonprofit business, including church organizations.

Pastors tend to take cover when financial pressures ensue;
instead they should take authority and take over. Conditions or
circumstances that bring about this stress must be defeated. If
you allow conditions or circumstances to take you over, you will
develop a phobia that will hinder you from becoming successful.
In order to remain on top of the situation, you need to introduce
certain practical steps to alleviate the financial distress.

1. ***Make sure that your income exceeds your spending.*** Due to
   low income, pastors find it difficult to stay above the fray
   with their finances. Where there is a low income, the pastor
   should negotiate a higher income. A pastor friend of mine is
   a university professor in the American Midwest. He told me
   that his salary was very low compared to his expenses. We
   both prayed about the situation. One afternoon the president

of the university asked my friend for a meeting. At the meeting my friend was informed of staff restructuring but assured
that he would not be impacted. He used the opportunity to
tender his request for salary adjustment. Seven days afterward, the president asked for another meeting, where the
professor was rewarded with a $30,000 pay increase. Praise
God! If you know what you need, you must route it through
God for provision of supernatural assistance.

2. *A budget is a solution, not a problem.* Many people throw
   the word "budget" around without a full comprehension
   of what it is and what it can accomplish. I believe that the
   moment you obtain a good understanding of budgeting,
   you will be encouraged to implement it. Here are some
   principles for creating an effective budget:

   • *A budget is a management tool that measures perfor-
     mance.* As a management tool, a budget looks at how
     budget managers perform. Each budget manager is held
     accountable for the resulting outcome of the budget.
     The outcome of the budget defines the next level for that
     manager. The manager is either promoted for good bud-
     get handling, or punished for mishandling the budget.
     My prayer is that the demon of mismanagement will be
     destroyed in the Name of Jesus. Amen!

   • *A budget provides guidance.* As a management tool (and a
     people tool), a budget gives guidance. The budget is the
     roadmap for every financial success. A man without a road-
     map normally does not do well. A roadmap is an impetus
     for success. It creates direction, and it provides navigation. It
     guides in times of difficulties. As the recession has come to
     an end, budgeting becomes the key player in your financial
     situation. Your budget tells you when to spend and when
     not to spend. It advises you to curtail unnecessary expenses.
     A person with a philanthropic mind is often tempted to
     overspend because those in need of help are always pulling

on him or her. Without this guiding tool, the philanthropist might be stuck in recession while others are prospering. Whenever there is a doubt in your financial circumstances, please endeavor to recheck your roadmap.

- *A budget stresses accountability.* A society in which no one is accountable is a society in chaos. A budget stresses accountability because someone needs to be held responsible for what has happened. In a family, there must be a discussion between husband and wife as to who should be responsible for the family budget. When this decision is made, if the family's finances prosper, the budget maker might be praised and rewarded with a family dinner or extra shopping money. On the other hand, if the budget fails, the responsible party gets blamed, and the family ends up with unnecessary strife. As we all know, money is an area the enemy uses to attack the family. As such, prudence is necessary for families to stay in harmony and remain together.

- *A budget is a control mechanism.* The budget becomes a tool that institutes discipline in people's lives. Whenever we say there is a control mechanism, we are really talking about allowing things to be in order. As a control point, the budget master must adhere to the standards of the budget. The budget master must not sway to the left or to the right. He must remain focused, disciplined, and directed. As a controlling tool, a budget becomes a mechanism for instituting error detection in the implementation process. When large variances show up in actual dollars versus budget dollars, you'll have a basis for good research.

- *A budget must provide realistic projections.* In the budgeting process, the budget master must learn to be candid in their projection. In many cases, the budget master may lose sight of the main picture and make unrealistic projections. This unrealistic projection brings the budget to its knees, creating financial chaos. In a period of financial pressure, you cannot operate in financial chaos. That is why it is important to follow the designed plans for your home and your small business.

3. Practical steps to surpluses.
   - *Consider forming a small business on the side,* especially if you are not called to a full-time ministry. When you seek the mind of the Holy Spirit, He will give you ideas on what to do. A friend shared with me how he started his retail computer business. He traveled to an East African nation and took 3 laptops with him. He was seeking business opportunities, and on that trip the 3 laptops were purchased by some customers. One of the customers asked for 24 laptops to be delivered in 60 days. My friend returned to Chicago and started putting the order together. Exhibit A, which follows, shows how my friend coordinated the new order and the amount of money he made.

# Exhibit A

### Detail Coordination of 24 Laptop Order (Including Margin Computation)

| Description | Unit Cost | Extension |
|---|---|---|
| Purchase of 24 laptops | $150 per laptop | $3,600.00 |
| Freight | $16 per laptop | $400.00 |
| Travel Ticket | $1,200 Roundtrip | $1,200.00 |
| Miscellaneous travel cost (Including hotel, meals, taxi, and tips) | | $800.00 |
| **Total Product & Travel Cost** | | **$6,000.00** |
| Sale of Each laptop | $400 | $9,600.00 |
| Refund on travel cost | | $2,400.00 |
| **Total Income Received** | | **$12,000.00** |
| **Margin/Gain $** | | **$6,000.00** |
| **Margin/Gain%** | | **100%** |

The idea is to find something unconventional to indulge in. The story continues, and my friend was invited by 4 schools to sell them laptops. You can imagine the rest of the story.

- *Consider forming a nonprofit business.* While the business described above is mainly geared toward making money, a nonprofit venture is designed NOT to make money or profit. A nonprofit venture that is well organized and run can yield lots of money because of the generosity of donors. Many nonprofit organizations stay afloat because the public shows their generosity in many ways through donation of money or goods that can be converted into cash. Here is an outline of the steps needed to establish a nonprofit organization:

## Creating a nonprofit organization

- Create Articles of Incorporation (sometimes called Certificate of Formation) and file with your specific state.

- Apply for EIN from the IRS (also called Tax ID Number or Federal Employee Identification Number).

- Create organizational bylaws.

- Prepare IRS Form 1023 or Form 1024, Application for Recognition of Exemption, including narrative of activities, financial projections and information, schedules, additional notes, and supplemental materials, especially if your organization has income greater than $50k.

## How to maintain nonprofit status

Many nonprofits lose their status for failing to file their 990, 990-EZ, or 990-N taxes.

- At year end, each nonprofit organization must file a tax return, except if the organization (e.g., a church) is exempt from filing based on how their 501c3 was formed. Each organization should prepare its financial statements and submit to its CPA to help file their 990, 990-EZ, or 990-N. If the nonprofit fails to file their taxes in 3 consecutive years, their 501c3 status will be revoked.

◦ Please note that reinstating a revoked 501c3 status is attainable but difficult.

## Advantages of owning a nonprofit organization

◦ Expenses can be tagged as nonprofit when completed.

◦ Monies to foundation/charity can be written off as charitable in the client's 1040.

◦ Monies donated to clients can be reported as charitable.

◦ Except for the initial application, no additional payment for 501c3 is required by the IRS for the life of the organization.

## Chapter 9

# WELLNESS

*"Beloved, I pray that all may go well with you and that you may be in good health, as it goes well with your soul." (3 John 2:2)*

Some time ago, I started having severe pains that literally spread throughout my entire body. I prayed earnestly, asking God to take the pain away. However, the pain persisted, and I had no choice but to visit my primary care physician. At first my doctor suspected arthritis, but after a series of X-rays and CT scans, he concluded that I had a disease called sarcoidosis. I looked him straight in his eyes and asked him, "What is sarcoidosis?" He informed me that it is an inflammatory disease that affects the lungs, eyes, joints, organs, and nervous system. Anticipating my next question, he added, "And there is no cure for it as of yet."

"So what can we do about the pains that travel all around my body?" I asked.

My doctor told me that I would have to rely upon pain medication moving forward, and that he had to refer me to a lung specialist because of abnormalities found on the CT scan.

Again, here I was—an evangelist who prays for others and has seen God heal all manner of sicknesses and diseases—faced with such devastating news.

My journey began March 5, 2008, at the Pulmonary Department. The lung specialist confirmed that my case was not as bad as it had looked on the CT scan. This news came as a big relief and of course I glorified "Abba Father," whom I had been calling upon to intervene. The lung issue set aside, I had to have my eyes checked by another specialist. I visited the ophthalmology department twice, on April 11 and September 15, 2008. All tests conducted came out well. However, the test on my sinuses did not. According to the specialist, the sarcoidosis affects my sinuses, and I was diagnosed with a chronic sinus condition that required immediate surgery.

Before any surgery, the pains traveling throughout my body suddenly left me. Praise God! However, I maintained annual follow-up appointments with the pulmonary and ophthalmology specialists. However, the otolaryngology (head and neck) appointments became more frequent. The sinus kept getting worse. Sometimes it was very difficult to breathe because of an excessive dry and bloody nose. Winter became a very difficult season. So, I had to be on both medication and sinus spray because I chose not to have the surgery. I will not forget the day I was leading a congregational prayer and my nose began to bleed. I held my nose and prayed to a hurried end to avoid embarrassment.

I am believing God for a miracle, and I know He will do it. Apart from the sarcoidosis issues, I realized that I was experiencing dizzy spells often. This continued until the Holy Spirit started leading me to teach wellness. As I studied, it dawned on me that changing my diet would impact my health in many positive ways. Wasting no time, I implemented a new, health-conscience regimen, to include more vegetables and fruits. Since I started on this new lifestyle, I have noticed that the constant dizziness left, and to my greatest surprise, my sinus condition improved drastically. I stopped taking medication but continued using the sinus spray. These changes in my diet helped me gain more strength than ever before.

My prayer life has also increased drastically, because I now wake up stronger and healthier. I know the improvements in my health are directly connected to the change in my diet because anytime I lose control and slip back into my old eating habits, mornings become a real struggle. In fact, there was a day I went to sleep earlier than normal, and I woke up later than usual. Observing my body, I felt weak and unwell. I have realized that whatever I put in my body determines how healthy and well I feel.

Unfortunately, many individuals, including pastors, have met untimely death because of poor personal healthcare. I wonder if some of those pastors would still be among us, fulfilling God's purposes in their lives, if they had focused more on their health. As we pray for pastors, it is crucial that we encourage them to manage their health, eat well, and exercise to keep their bodies strong. Ignorance has taken more lives than the devil himself: "My people are destroyed for lack of knowledge; because you have rejected knowledge" (Hosea 4:6a).

## Preventive Measures

Prevention, they say, is better than cure. I struggled to write this chapter because I still battle with the chronic sinus issue caused by sarcoidosis. It is one area in my life I would have preferred to share after experiencing total victory. However, I chose to share it here for pastors to understand that prevention and taking care of the body is vital for the course of their assignment. I am very passionate about this chapter because the devil has introduced a lot of deceit to the body of Christ. I know of pastors who have taken healing power to an extreme. Unfortunately, some rely on God to heal those in their congregations, and teach this accordingly. However, those same pastors may not encourage their parishioners to visit their doctors to be properly informed of their health conditions.

I, too, believe in the healing power of God. As an intercessor, I have learned that praying specifically is important when asking God to heal. Using myself as an example, I needed to know the name of the condition, sarcoidosis, in order to pray correct prayers for the healing I received. I had to know the facts of my health, but I did not allow those facts, shared by my doctor and specialists, to determine my truth. Acknowledging facts does not cause one to lose faith. Though facts exist, you and I know the truth. The truth is that by His stripes we are healed! I do not suggest that any minister of God deny facts and say they are walking in faith. That is deception from the pit of hell. Know the facts and fight the good fight of faith, and the truth will manifest.

I have a friend who was diagnosed with high blood pressure. He accepted that fact and used the prescribed medications. Studying an article on healthy eating, he acquired new knowledge on eating properly. He started eating a balanced diet: more organic fresh fruits and vegetables, whole grains, lean protein, and low-fat dairy. He also reduced sodium by cutting down on his salt intake. His high blood pressure left for good. Today, he's on a mission, working to serve God and fulfilling his purpose without struggling any more with high blood pressure.

Knowing how important this chapter is, I was privileged to have two medical professionals contribute. Please, as you read, I do hope you will consider your personal health, as well as your pastor's health. The information shared below is not intended to be all-inclusive nor address individual health concerns. I strongly recommend consulting your doctor regarding your health and any dietary changes.

★★★

*Dr. Onyinye Enyia Daniel is the senior manager of Health Informatics Analysis at Blue Cross Blue Shield of Illinois and an adjunct instructor at the University of Illinois School of Public Health, Department of Health Policy and Administration.*

Pastors are typically the main point of contact when church members are experiencing periods of crisis. Both the unpredictability and the serious nature of many issues necessitates focus and stamina to deal with myriad issues among the congregation. Mental and physical health are essential to the well-being and purposeful support of any pastor and his or her ministry. The Substance Abuse and Mental Health Services Administration estimates that almost one in five Americans suffer from some form of mental illness each year (SAMHSA, 2017). Pastors are not exempt from these statistics. As such, it is critical that pastoral support teams have solid, clear policies or guidelines to support both the pastor's mental health and physical health.

Pastoring has many immeasurable rewards, and can be incredibly fulfilling. However, pastors are placed in the midst of high-tension, high-stress situations, sometimes for prolonged periods of time. These high-stress circumstances can have adverse implications for health. Studies have shown that prolonged stress is a contributing risk factor for several morbidities, such as high blood pressure (hypertension), and can indirectly contribute to risk factors that further contribute to hypertension, such as poor diet and inadequate physical activity (American Heart Association, 2017). Mental health is inextricably linked to physical health, and effective stress management has positive implications for both. From a biblical perspective, 1 Thessalonians 5:16-18 states, "Rejoice always, pray continually, give thanks in all circumstances, for this is God's will for you in Christ Jesus."

This verse is particularly salient in that it encourages us to give thanks, despite our circumstances. Even in the midst of high-stress situations, we are encouraged to give thanks and rejoice. Keeping this in mind, the following are effective tools to encourage pastoral mental wellness and emotional health:

1. Set aside time each week to rest. This time should not be spent fielding requests from church members, or completing tasks. Rather, this is a time for introspection and the inward expression of gratitude and thankfulness for God's goodness and mercy. Pastoral support should work diligently to encourage and protect this time for the pastor. Often it may be difficult for pastors, who are so used to pouring into others, to adhere to this boundary. Those surrounding the pastor should emphasize this time for the pastor to rest and rejuvenate mentally and emotionally. While the duration of such time is arbitrary and depends on the needs of the pastor, clear boundaries should be set—even, if necessary, codified in ministry documents or policies.

2. The pastor's support team must emphasize and encourage time for the pastor to spend with his or her spouse. The intimate relationship between spouses is one of encouragement, openness, and oneness, where a pastor can share his deepest emotions, hopes, and dreams. A married pastor must have an outlet in his or her spouse to share and talk through the things that may weigh upon his or her heart. This deep sharing promotes a healthy family relationship, while allowing for personal expressions of emotion in a safe, secure environment. Freedom to express oneself in a Godly, safe space is critical to pastoral emotional and mental well-being. In addition, peer-to-peer support groups may prove useful for pastors as a safe environment to both receive and provide support, counseling, and fellowship with others who may share similar experiences.

3. If possible, delegate tasks to qualified and appropriate laborers in the church. Burnout can be a major issue, particularly for pastors who find it difficult to maintain boundaries around personal rest, or who have difficulty saying "No." Effective delegation of appropriate tasks and

responsibilities to leaders in the church can help lighten the load and can help mitigate issues associated with burnout.

4. Pastors should be encouraged to see a physician regularly for general health checkups and to monitor his/her health. Regular checkups should be a top priority, with time set aside at regular intervals. In addition, psychiatric services should be encouraged for mental health issues.

5. Pastors should engage in regular physical activity. The American Heart Association recommends 30 minutes or more of physical activity on most days of the week to maintain optimal health. Physical activity can include walking, jogging, swimming, playing a team sport, or other activities that elevate the heart rate.

6. Encourage a healthful diet and the intake of adequate fluid. Pastors should be encouraged to follow current healthy dietary guidelines, which include nutritious options to promote health and wellness. A healthful diet sets the stage for disease prevention and provides the energy and nutrients needed to handle everyday stress.

Overall, the measures suggested provide a set of guidelines for pastoral support teams to encourage practical and well-rounded support and encouragement for our pastors, and should be prayerfully and purposefully considered.

American Heart Association (2017). *Managing Stress to Control High Blood Pressure.*

Substance Abuse and Mental Health Association (2017). https://www.samhsa.gov.

★★★

*Dr. Anene Ositadinma, MB, BS, is a family physician in Woodbury, Minnesota.*

Men and women, irrespective of their age, occupation or ethnicity, are faced with the same health challenges—though different based on their gender. Pastors are in the same category but are uniquely different because of the nature of their work and position. Pastors are human but expected to be spiritual by their knowledge of and faith in God; as a result they should not be ill. This is far from the truth. Yes, pastors minister, pray, and lay hands on the sick. With faith and God's grace there is healing on occasions. This unwittingly puts a lot pressure on pastors, to the extent that they may have the expectation that their physical body is above illness and may not take care of themselves. Inasmuch as pastors are servants of God, standing between man and Christ who is our intermediary with Almighty God, they are still human. Being human, their bodies are also under the physical laws of nature. So pastors will pray, and God will answer and heal according to His will. But this does not mean that pastors should not take care of their health.

I have tried to go through the basic healthcare needs for men and women as they apply to preventive care as well as treatment needs. For easier understanding, I will separate the healthcare needs into two categories: Healthcare Maintenance and Health Diagnosis.

## Healthcare Maintenance

Maintenance is a way of preventing future healthcare complications by being proactive in seeking and managing our life risks. The doctor does screening laboratory tests as well as counseling at these visits. The body and organs undergo wear and tear, and we may or may not have certain things in life that impact us negatively or positively either at current times or in the future. It is known that prevention is better than cure. There are a lot of preventable illness around us. Take, for example, heart disease and stroke. It is known that lifestyle issues like increased weight with lack of exercise (a sedentary lifestyle) and poor dietary choices are associated with heart disease and stroke, through causes like diabetes mellitus, increased blood pressure, and elevated cholesterol. These do not have warning symptoms earlier but may cause late complications. In our busy lives, especially pastors' lives, the symptoms may be covered up or explained as too much engagement, until the complications take the person to the ER. But having to annual or bi-annual visits to the doctor for healthcare maintenance presents opportunity to discover risks that may otherwise lead to these health disasters.

In addition to screening for factors such as heart disease risks, the health maintenance visit affords the opportunity for screening for cancers, as well as discussions of lifestyle behaviors that may impact increase in cancers. Cancers that at this time can be screened for with high confidence of success include colon cancer, breast cancer, skin cancer, testicular cancer, cervical cancer, and others. Different procedures are used for these screenings, and screening may not be ideal for certain other cancers and are not recommended—but it takes a visit to the physician to discuss this and find out what screening is best for individuals.

Last but not least, healthcare maintenance includes things like making sure that one has gotten the necessary immunizations for disease prevention at the various ages and stages of life. There is a list of immunizations for adults included.

## Health Care Maintenance: Physical Exams Based on Age

1. **Age 20–40.** Screening for risks of heart disease and discussion of family history, as well as lifestyle behaviors changes or maintenance geared toward having a healthy life presently and making sure that it continues into older ages. At this age the cancers for screening are mainly skin, cervical, testicular, and the beginning of breast cancer screening. This is mostly encouraging and teaching

individuals to be aware of skin moles and make sure to be knowledgeable about their body, especially the testicles, in men. Women will have cervical cancer screenings and discuss breast cancer screening and get the first mammogram.

2. **Age 41–50.** By this age, in addition to #1 above, discussion about prostate screening in men begins. (Of note, prostate screening is somewhat controversial, so discussion with the doctor is encouraged so one will understand the needs.) Colon cancer screening begins at 50 years, except if there is family history, in which case earlier screening is done. For women, breast cancer screening with a mammogram and cervical cancer screening continues.

3. **Age 51–70.** Continue 1 and 2 above. However, making sure screenings are done according to the recommended timeline is key in this age range.

4. **Ages 70 and above.** Screenings will continue well into the 80s and 90s as long it is the wish of the patient, although some cancer screenings may be not worthwhile doing. This needs to be discussed with the healthcare provider.

Most of these visits will be at most 40–60 minutes of the day, and the advice is not to bring urgent medical problems to a general wellness check, so that the provider can spend the time discussing healthcare maintenance with the patient. Schedule a special visit when you notice an unusual medical issue.

## Clinical Diagnoses

Clinical diagnoses are medical diagnoses affecting individuals for which they receive consistent treatments and may expect to be seen by their doctors at intervals for good care and follow-up. These include—but are definitely not limited to—the following:

Mental health issues, hypertension (high blood pressure, HTN), hyperlipidemia (high cholesterol), diabetes mellitus type 2, arthritis and musculoskeletal issues, asthma or chronic lung disease, enlarged prostate (BPH), erectile dysfunction or other sexual issues, headaches, abdominal ulcers, vision problems, menstrual issues in women.

The list is almost inexhaustible. I will dwell on the ones that are most common.

## Mental Health

### Depression/Anxiety

Though not physical ailments but psychological, sometimes with physical symptoms, these are an issue with attached social stigma, making it hard for pastors to seek help for them. Depression and anxiety, unfortunately, are thought of as purely spiritual by some people, so it may be believed that pastors should not struggle with these issues. Thus it becomes difficult for pastors who have symptoms of depression or anxiety to seek help.

There is a misunderstanding that, although these may be psychological, it is also spiritual and a manifestation of demonic attacks. This is possible, but scientifically speaking, the current understanding is that an imbalance in some neurotransmitters is implicated in depression/anxiety and the entities associated with them. Replacing these neurotransmitters using medication is usually the treatment. Additionally, treatments such as psychological therapy or counseling are known to be very effective.

Depression usually manifests with several symptoms, but the two most common are anhedonia and moodiness. Anhedonia means inability to find joy in activities that one used to enjoy. There may be irritability, or feeling unworthy of oneself or others. There may be too much or not enough eating or sleeping. There is fear of impending doom.

Symptoms of anxiety include heightened worry and difficulty stopping worrying. Persons with anxiety also get irritable easily.

In both depression and anxiety, there may be concentration difficulties. Substance abuse may become a way out for some people; although substance use may seem effective, it will ultimately make them more depressed and anxious.

Depression and anxiety often respond very well to treatment, whether prescribed medications or working with a therapist to figure out what could be the cause of the issues. Just discussing the issues with a primary care provider often makes the patient feel better.

## Other Mental Health Issues

Problems such as attention deficit disorder, post-traumatic stress disorder, and social anxiety are also associated with anxiety and depression.

There are many mental illnesses, and most or all of them can be treated in various ways, including prayer. However, it is good to seek professional help in addition to spiritual help—if not to prescribe treatment, at least to be a guide to help along the way, with respect to one's spiritual needs.

## Physical Health

One area of health that is often neglected or ignored has to do with sexual problems. Pastors are human and do have needs for affection, both physically and emotionally. Sometimes toward the later years of life, there is a reduction in hormones; this is especially pronounced in women but also occurs in men and usually leads to reduced libido and then to inability to be affectionate and close to their spouses. This may lead to difficulty in the marriage and stress in the home. Men may have erectile dysfunction, while women in menopause may start to feel aversion to the physical needs of their husbands. There is usually help and treatment, and these issues should not waved aside. Seek help and discuss this with your medical provider.

Medical diagnoses like diabetes mellitus, hypertension, high cholesterol, obesity, and others, are progressive if not caught on time. For one who does not visit or even have a healthcare provider, this poses a very high risk. So once again, it is necessary to visit your healthcare provider at regular intervals to diagnose and manage these issues.

Other clinical problems, as noted above, that require regular visits as followup are also very important. For all prolonged or chronic medical problems, the key is to make sure that treatment is supplied where it can be and that good control be achieved. When it is not possible to cure or control the disease, a doctor's task is to make sure the individual is comfortable and symptoms reduced enough in order for the individual to function fully.

In summary, pastors are human. They have a physical body which is affected by medical issues just like everyone else. It is necessary for both pastors and and their congregations to be aware of this and help the pastor achieve optimal health. It is known that a majority of medical ailments, including some cancers, are linked to our lifestyle, especially exercise and diet—so we need to be able to create time and work on the body, as our Heavenly Father would have us do, to keep it healthy and ourselves happy.

# CONCLUSION

*"Brothers, pray for us." (1 Thessalonians 5:25)*

Having read to the end, either as a pastor or a congregant, you can surely agree with me that pastors need prayer. The church should cultivate the habit of praying and interceding for their local pastors. Pastors need our prayers, just as we needed them to be praying for us.

In the game of football, the players are on the field, running the plays of their coaches. Those on the sidelines and in the bleachers often direct the players, shouting demands and directions that cannot be heard. We must realize that the view of the game is different for the players on the field than it is for the spectators who are not on the field. So be careful condemning and gossiping about your pastor. Having answered the call, he is on the field, running God's plays, seeing them from a view different from ours. Everyone needs to get on the field and become involved. Do not be a spectator, but collectively build the church or the ministry with your leader.

For you, pastors, I encourage you to connect with one another, either in a small group or on a larger scale, to be accountable to one another. No one can be an island. Regardless of the grace upon your life regarding your success in ministry, Pastor, you still need a gathering of like-minded brethren. Never get to a stage where you feel you do not need prayers or counsel from others. As much grace as was upon the life of Paul, even he requested prayers (1 Thessalonians 5:25).

This is my prayer for pastors and leaders:

> May the Lord open the floodgates of heaven and rain down fresh anointing for a new beginning. May He give you more grace to overcome trials and temptations, strength to overcome weaknesses, wisdom to lead, a large heart to tolerate and to forgive offenders, and wisdom to balance the family and ministry. I pray for you the power to resist every attack from the kingdom of darkness, authority to preach the gospel without compromise, and, above all, for God's goodness and mercy to follow all the pastors and ministers now and forever more. Amen!

Pause a moment and pray for your pastor and for all the pastors and leaders who are serving in various ministries. Pray especially for the pastors who have fallen or walked away from their assignment, or who are discouraged. Pray that they be strong and courageous.

I end this book with prayers contributed by many intercessors who read this book and indeed dedicated their time to prayer for pastors. Those who are not praying yet, by His grace, may begin to pray for their pastor after reading this book. So, Pastor, there is no reason to fail God. Stay humble and soar like an eagle! God be with you.

—Brother Fredrick Ezeji-Okoye

# INTERCESSORS' PRAYERS FOR PASTORS AND MINISTERS
*Contributed by Carol-Ann Abraham*

Lord, thank you so much for the wisdom imparted through this book, the revelation of who you are, and how your hand is in every situation. I thank you for the gift of our pastors to the church. I ask for Holy Spirit intervention as people read this book, to get the insight and information you want them to have, as well as to have personal encounters with you. I ask for favor in distribution, so that this book will land in the hands of those you've already prepared to read it and be touched by it. I thank you that there is a field of intercessors out there who will read this book and be moved to intercede at a higher level for their pastors. I thank you for the pastors who will read this book and be encouraged in their faith and ministry through the support evident through this book. I thank you for those who are called to the ministry, who will adequately seek you for their clear calling before stepping into any particular role, so that they will be where you want them to be, doing what you've called them to do, under the grace you have for them there.

I thank you for the clarity regarding challenges of pastoring that will allow those stepping freshly into ministry to be prepared for the potential problems ahead. I thank you for the unity this book will bring to the body to stand behind, support, and lift up their pastors in prayer and to have a unanimous agreement of its importance. I thank you for the prayer teams that will set time aside specifically to pray for pastors, to cover them and support them in this way, and I thank you for the leaders you've chosen to minister specifically to pastors and give them a safe place of prayer, ministry, support, and respite to be refreshed and rejuvenated.

Thank you, Lord, for the angelic protection you're releasing even now over pastors in this season. I see a hedge of protection around them, and for that I thank you! I thank you, Lord, for the release you're giving pastors from the pressure of appearance. Allow them to more freely be vulnerable with their personal struggles and bring freedom from appearing to "have it all together," or "have the perfect family." Thank you for the protection you're placing on pastors' families and their marriages. And I thank you, Lord, that the church will stand together and fight to protect the marriages and families of pastors. I thank you for bringing freedom and release from perfectionism and control that will allow pastors to be genuinely human in front of their congregations. And I thank you for a new generation of congregants that not only accepts this, but demands it of their pastors. Pull pastors into closer relationship with those in their congregations, leadership, and community. Allow them the freedom to socialize, without pretense or façade and without impure motives of those with which they socialize. Bring a new level of humanity to the image of the pastor through the eyes of the church.

I thank you for the increased anointing, the grace upon grace for the calling of pastors to fulfill the vision you've given each of them. Thank you for a release of strategy and provision for the vision in this hour. I thank you for a rising church, led by your chosen pastors and even a flushing out of those that aren't in their proper position. Please bless your pastors with support, wisdom, abundance, and rest. I thank you for the rest upon pastors as they relinquish the need to perform or hold up appearances that has been wrongfully placed on them by the church.

Please bring healing to those who are holding past hurts or resentment, and release a flood of forgiveness. Thank you for your healing balm upon them. Thank you for healing the wounds that pastors have taken from misdirected accusations, expectations, and misunderstanding from current and past congregants. I ask you to bring healing to all those wounded by the church, whether pastors, leaders, or otherwise. Heal your church, Lord, and bring a new level of unity.

Thank you, Lord, for a renewed and refreshed focus on Jesus, growing closer to Him with each and every day, and a surrender that allows the Holy Spirit to do a transformative work in each and every one of us. I ask you to pour blessing upon blessing onto each person that reads this book as they capture the full message you want them to take from it. I thank you also for the provision and direction in publishing, releasing, and distributing the book so that it may reach all the places you've already planned. We love you, Lord, and release this book into your hands. Do with it what you desire. In Jesus' name. Amen.

★★★

*Contributed by Heiker Bauer*

Heavenly Father, I'm praying for all pastors, ministers, and leaders in the body of Christ, that you touch their spirits, souls, and bodies. Fill them with your Spirit, connect them with you in a heartfelt way, transform their lives, and fill them with your Word. Help them fulfill their purposes, live their kingdom assignments, and walk in your kingdom ways. Reveal to them your mysteries. Change their lives so that there is no difference between your will and theirs. Give them your righteousness, your peace, and your joy to fulfill their purposes. Let them walk in your love and grace. Protect them from everything that can hold them back from their kingdom assignments. In Jesus' mighty and marvelous name. Amen.

★★★

*Contributed by Ella Lameyer*

Dear Heavenly Father,

We praise you for your gracious, unmeasurable love, which you have poured out through Jesus Christ's death and resurrection. Lord, may we ever abide in your presence, for that is where we find peace and overwhelming joy. Thank you, Jesus, for being our Advocate and Defense, for we are your beloved. Warrior of the Ages, renew our vision where it is out of line, and where it is in order send divine connections to assist in the work of your Kingdom. May we fight valiantly for truth and resist falsehood with love and justice.

Thank you, Father, for each valley and mountain which is refining our character and drawing us ever closer to you. Lord, when we are far, pull us near to your cleansing blood, our defense. Holy Spirit, when we are close, enable us to remain open to your movements with hands of surrender and service. Holy Spirit, be our refreshment and provider. As you refresh us, we will share our stories and even our very lives with those whom you have allowed us to mentor, lead, and serve.

Shepherd of our souls, may we be led by you alone rather than by the desires of this world, which beckon to us for temporary pleasure and significance. May every other desire fade in comparison as we recognize that we are your beloved Bride, and that our identity is rooted at the cross where your blood was shed for our forgiveness. Help us to daily step into the reality that we are forgiven, children of the King. For we are no longer bound, dead, nor broken, but alive and walking in freedom.

Thank you, Holy Spirit, for the spiritual journey upon which we are embarking. May we accept your ongoing invitation to be active in our lives. As we show forth your glory, stop us when we are becoming either too self-focused or too short-sighted. Finally, thank you, Lord, that we are in the process of being refined over time and through your purposes, to achieve your best results. God, help us to learn how to weep with those who are mourning and rejoice with those who are celebrating.

We wait expectantly for all that you have for us in this next season, regardless whether it is winter or summer, spring or fall. We choose today to return with testimonies of your favor, protection, and faithfulness. In Jesus' name. Amen.

★★★

### Contributed by Ramon Samaniego

I declare the blessing of the Lord on you right now, pastors, in the name of Jesus. I'm holding Him according to His word 1 Timothy 5:17: "Let the elders who rule well be considered worthy of double honor, especially those who labor in preaching and teaching." This is also my prayer for you, pastors, according to the word of God.

**Numbers 6:24–26:** "May the Lord bless you, and protect you. May the Lord smile on you and be gracious to you. May the Lord show you HIS FAVOR and give you His peace." Amen.

★★★

### Contributed by Ophelia Quaindo

**1 Peter 5:8:** LORD, I pray a prayer of protection for every single pastor around the world. I pray that you will protect all pastors from every demonic attack of Satan. LORD, give them the strength to endure temptation and stand firm against every accusation of the enemy. Help them stand firm in your service, for your people, and for their faith as well.

**James 1:14–15:** LORD, I pray for the spirit of purity over our pastors. Please protect them from every power of sin that will try to take hold of them. Guard their hearts against sin and keep their consciences clean and pure. May you keep them close to you and grant them the grace to always abide by your word.

**Romans 1:11–12:** LORD, I pray for the spirit of encouragement for our pastors. Let their spirits be refreshed with the love of Christ and by the power of your Spirit. Help them keep their faith and continue pressing on, regardless of life's pressures and every contention they may be facing.

**James 1:5:** LORD, I pray for wisdom for our pastors. As Solomon asked for wisdom and you granted unto him, I pray for a double portion of that wisdom for them. Grant them wisdom in all they do. May you help them to know your ways and where to go when the way is not clear; for your ways are not our ways, neither your thoughts our thoughts. LORD, grant them the spirit of discernment to know right from evil and to be able to apply your word even to the most confusing and challenging situations.

★★★

### *Contributed by Peace Udechukwu*

Heavenly Father, you have ordered the function of the five-fold ministry according to Ephesians 4:11–12 to be in place for the edification of the body of Christ, so I declare, Heavenly Father, that you thrust out these gifts in the body like never before. I ask that you equip the various churches with the knowledge and understanding of the purpose for the five-fold ministry so that your will shall be done. Pour out your grace on every ministry leader that you have called into your fold. Equip them with the five-fold leaders and enlarge them with your wisdom, knowledge, courage, and understanding to do your will. Let your mercy rain upon them and your grace sustain them. Lead them according to your will so that none may fall into the traps of the enemy.

Heavenly Father, it has been revealed to your servants that unforgiveness dries up the anointing and gives birth to spiritual cancer. Father, I ask that you open the eyes of understanding of this revelation to pastors and minsters of your word. Let them be filled and overflowing with the fruits of the spirit, that the overflow may impact those around them. Strengthen the wills of pastors and ministers, that they will desire your will above their own; release in them a drive to seek your unadulterated truth. Give them wisdom in times of trials and the peace that passeth all understanding.

Heavenly Father, you are the Alpha and Omega, and we honor you for who you are. We know that your loving kindness is eternal and your mercies are forever. Help us to be more like you, and purge us from transgressions that separate us from you. Instill in us a burning desire to know more about you and your will for your church. Holy Spirit, guide us in the way we should go daily, that we may not depart from the will of God. Our life is in your hands, Heavenly Father, and we submit to you now and always. In Jesus' name. Amen.

★★★

*Contributed by Ijeoma Ezeji-Okoye*

**Proverbs 16:18:** Father, I pray for every pastor, that the spirit of pride be destroyed and pulled down in their lives, so that they experience your glory and manifestation of your presence in their homes, ministry, and all that concerns them. In Jesus' name. Amen.

**2 Corinthians 12:8–9:** Father, I pray for more grace in the lives of every pastor, that no matter the situation or circumstance, they will not give up. Father, uphold every pastor with your right hand of righteousness, make a way of escape for them, restore

all they have lost, and above all, keep them from sin-
ning against you. In Jesus' name. Amen.

**Psalm 51:10:** Father, I pray for every pastor who,
one way or another, has missed the mark, acted on their
own will, or gone astray through the lust of this world.
Lord, I pray in your infinite mercy that you divinely visit
that pastor, and let him or her experience your touch and
love once again. In Jesus' name. Amen.

# ABOUT THE AUTHOR

Fredrick K. Ezeji-Okoye is a communicator at heart with a passion to share the Gospel both orally and in wrting. Among his many gifts and talents, he is a minister, writer, and motivational speaker with a mandate to equip and empower the body of Christ by igniting a greater thirst and hunger for God's word and intercessory prayer.

He is the founder and president of "The Men of Faith Network," a fast-growing diverse, and multicultural network of pastors and leaders with global outreach. Fredrick is the CEO of The Liberty Foundation LLC, a company that specializes in training church workers and consultants.

He resides in the Chicago metro area with his wife Ijeoma and their three children, Chisom, Nkiruka, and Chinenye.

www.libertyfoundationllc.com
www.menoffaithnetwork.org

www.ingramcontent.com/pod-product-compliance
Lightning Source LLC
Jackson TN
JSHW011950131224
75386JS00042B/1654